CW00326472

An Indian Summer

James Cameron started his lifelong career in journalism in Dundee in 1928. After leaving Scotland he travelled widely as a foreign correspondent in almost every part of the world, working for *Picture Post* and the ill-fated *News Chronicle* before becoming a freelance.

He won the Granada Journalist of the Year Award and Foreign Correspondent of the Decade Award for his journalism, and he moved on to television journalism in the 1970s.

James Cameron, who wrote several other books, including *Point of Departure*, died in 1985. The *Observer* said of his work: 'There are very few journalists capable of the precise combination of topicality, experience and controlled indignation which make up his best pieces.' *The Times*, writing about *An Indian Summer*, described it as 'The diary of a year in the life of a sharp and sensitive man spent in various Indian settings . . . Delightful pages that evoke everything of the odd pattern of human behaviour under the Indian sun'. The *Times of India* was equally complimentary: 'Few foreigners are so well qualified to write a book on India . . . It is no exaggeration to say that he is in love with this vast, complex, confusing and often tormenting country.'

By the same author

TOUCH OF THE SUN

MANDARIN RED

1914

THE AFRICAN REVOLUTION

1916

WITNESS

POINT OF DEPARTURE

WHAT A WAY TO RUN THE TRIBE
(Selected Journalism)

JAMES CAMERON

An Indian Summer

PENGUIN BOOKS

PENGUIN BOOKS

Published by the Penguin Group
27 Wrights Lane, London w8 5TZ, England
Viking Penguin Inc., 40 West 23rd Street, New York, New York 10010, USA
Penguin Books Australia Ltd, Ringwood, Victoria, Australia
Penguin Books Canada Ltd, 2801 John Street, Markham, Ontario, Canada L3R 1B4
Penguin Books (NZ) Ltd, 182–190 Wairau Road, Auckland 10, New Zealand

Penguin Books Ltd, Registered Offices: Harmondsworth, Middlesex, England

First published by Macmillan London Ltd 1974
Published in Penguin Books 1987
Reprinted 1987 (twice), 1988

Printed and bound in Great Britain by
Cox & Wyman Ltd, Reading

Foreword

THIS WAS originally conceived more than three years ago as a book about India, which I have known and perversely loved for a long time. I had a feeling even then that there had been more than enough books about India.

By the time I began, however, I was married to an Indian; it produced a wholly new dimension to the job and dispelled my doubts. It is in the book that 'if I were to seek pride in India now it would in a tiny way be part of my pride; if there were to be disappointment and regret I must now share that regret, and in some oblique way accept its responsibility'.

In this book I have said things which may sound critical, wounding, even angry. In expiation I can say that I have been as bitter about many societies, including my own. I do not mean to be hurtful to a warm and generous people who have never been other than kind to me; wherein I have seen things cruel and hostile it is because they are cruel and hostile to India itself. Only now, after twenty-five years of knowing India, can I make the presumption of claiming a small share both in its rare joys and its frequent sorrows.

But of course that last Indian Summer was not allowed to be enough. The Bangladesh episode intervened. Foolishly, perhaps, I went up to pry; I was badly injured on the Border. I spent a long time in hospitals in London, where a pretty full and exacting life at last caught up with me and sent me into the strange realms of profound heart-surgery, and the strangely changed world that follows it.

There are after all two meanings to An Indian Summer, and by and by for me they merged into one.

This is why I dedicate this book to an Indian.

1

I HAD seen the collision coming, but when it happened the impact was so abrupt and stunning that it shocked the sense out of me, and for a while I sat quietly among the broken glass of the jeep as though I had been sitting there forever. In any case I found I could not move because of the dead weight of the soldiers on either side of me. We had hit the bus head-on. The front of the jeep was embedded under its bonnet, and the crash must have somehow distorted the wiring apparatus because the first thing I became aware of was a continuous metallic howl from the horn that nobody tried to stop. It seemed as though the machinery itself was screaming in pain, while all the people involved were spellbound and silent.

The first rains of the monsoon were streaking vertically out of the low grey sky like a curtain, and through the cataract along the roadside came the procession of refugees: gaunt, drenched, wordless, totally abstracted, driving their fatigue and apathy along in an interminable caravan through the soggy mud of the road into India. The rain was almost opaque. The Bengalis glanced without expression or wonder at the mangled wreckage of the jeep and the bus, but they did not pause nor question it; why should they? They had been four or five days on the road from East Pakistan, hiding from the Punjabi soldiers from the West; they were now quite drained of emotion or response. We offered no threat; they offered no help. In my inertia it all seemed very reasonable. I felt I had been watching just such a frieze of refugees for the last twenty years, and I was just bewildered enough to have a momentary difficulty in recalling where I was – Germany, Palestine, Vietnam, even India itself, so long ago? Refugees are the last International.

This multitude was pouring out from what was not quite yet Bangladesh. Already some four or five million had crossed over, and still they were coming at the rate of about sixty thousand a day, ragged and silent, carrying on their backs their very young and very old, anaesthetised by exhaustion and despair. There was no noise, no complaint, no kind of tumult. Now, on their last lap to the camps, the rains were overwhelming them. Ten minutes earlier we had passed three babies drowned and abandoned in the few inches of rushing rainwater by the road. Our small personal disaster was of no consequence to the Pakistanis now. I wondered how I was ever going to move again.

Some of the passengers from the stranded bus had climbed out and now stood grouped around the wreck with the mute incurious Indian stare, doing nothing.

Suddenly the braying horn stopped, and then there was nothing to hear but the thudding rain.

Sitting there wedged in the front of the jeep I found at first that I could hardly stir. The driver to my left was apparently dead; the Colonel on my right seemed nearly so; they were both big and corpulent men and they lolled against me, jamming me between their khaki tunics and spilling blood into my lap. The Colonel's face was a makeup of fantasy; he had been scalped, and as fast as the wound soaked him scarlet the rains washed away the blood and diluted it; the broken jeep stood in a red pool that turned pink and drained away into the mud.

After a while I dragged myself out from between the

8

Colonel and the subhadar, but I found that I could not stand at all, and was obliged to sit against the back wheel in the sludge. The refugees walked slowly around me, patiently plodding west.

By and by a police truck came by and helped me into Krishnanagar, and from there another truck lifted me the ninety miles back to Calcutta. It was not a smooth road and by now the pain was very bad. I had two broken legs and a small dislocation of the spine. Or rather I thought that was all I had.

In the months to come, lying in a London ward with a divided sternum and an electric heart I had much time to reflect on the irony that I had been projected into my new *avatar*, not inappropriately, in India.

I was rather amateurishly strapped together and shipped back on the plane to London, though I recall little of the journey. It was a curious way to end a honeymoon.

For that matter it had been an odd way to begin it.

2

WHY DO I come, I wonder; why am I here? For twenty-five
years I have been asking, at this first fatigued moment in
the steaming heat of the Indian dawn, this first encounter
with the opaque evasive velvet official eyes – why must I
return to this tormented, confused, corrupt, futile and exasperating place as though I loved it, as though I needed
it, as though I had to be forever reminded of its hopelessness and the splendour of its sorrow?

Yet if I ask this question, why then, when I am not
there, do I miss it so? Each time I arrive my heart so
quickly sinks, yet each time I leave India I know there is
something of me I have left behind, some final question to
ask, something I have not understood or unjustly condemned, some service that is owed to me or that I have
left undone – I must return to India's cruelties and follies
and enchantments, so that I can recall the days of my own
innocence and that first surrender to the smell of the lamp.
There is no sense to it. And yet now for the first time
there was more than sense, there was compulsion; I had a
stake here now.

I was now married to an Indian; I was now bodily and
mentally part of this scene in a way I never was before.
Nothing in the aspects of my marriage added anything
tangible to an experience of India slowly and awkwardly
and imperfectly acquired over so many years, and yet it
added everything. A right to be here that I had never

felt in the British days nor thereafter, this I could now tentatively claim. If I were to seek pride in India now it would in a tiny way be part of my pride; if there were to be disappointment and regret I must now share that regret, and in some oblique way accept its responsibility. For twenty-five years I had been a repetitive stranger in India; this I was no longer, nor ever could be again. The wife at my side had it all as her birthright, the wondrous and the terrible, but as I had given her my name she had made a greater gift to me of her own one five-hundred millionth portion of her inheritance. If I had loved India once I must now love it otherwise, and with a changed emphasis; if I recoiled from its horrors I must no longer claim immunity, and my protest could no longer be made from the out-sider's privilege I had used so long. It was a wholly imagin-ary and romantic transfiguration, and indeed somehow pre-tentious, but it gave me enormous pleasure to consider it – here, entering Bombay in my new role, trying where I could to see everything before me with a new pair of eyes.

Some obscure natural law ordains that one must arrive at Bombay always just before daybreak: dark and heavy sunless heat, like the breath from a laundry, dishevelment, the grey dust of drying concrete. Santa Cruz in Bombay is like every airport on earth, forever half-built, tentative, forever littered with planks and temporary footholds, en-gaged in the endless business of expanding for the traffic of the future by upsetting the amenities of the present. Airports are like restless, troublesome housewives, eter-nally adjusting the furniture to prepare for the morrow. In India they are the only institutions without a sense of continuity. Yet the modifications were fitful and half-hearted, the spilled cement lay petrified on the floor, the temporary hardboard walls stayed on and on, institutional-ising themselves, the scaffolding and trestles became part of the mis-en-scène; it was like being backstage at a play that had been running for years. Fourteen hours ago we had left London airport, a masterpiece of ill-considered and inconvenient design smugly settled and established in its bright supermarket polish; now we were in a place which was apparently growing organically, as the mood took it.

I was briefly seized by the sudden unreasonable happiness that comes to me with the steamy touch of India in the early hours, the khaki-clad porters roused from sleep, already contending shrilly at their first waking breath, the smells of spice and disinfectant, the sight of tin trunks and bedrolls, the family parties gathered with garlands to welcome the drowsy relative from the West, above all the embracing heat. Even the certainty of problems and frustrations to come gave me a feeling of assurance: they had not happened yet, meanwhile I was content to be back.

I do not know how many times I had made this landfall, certainly almost every year, and sometimes oftener, since that first time when the flags and uniforms had been British (but so soon to change) when the air was full of equivocation and doubt, and the walls scrawled with the words 'Quit India' – under which many an embittered British squaddie wrote his addendum: 'I Wish I Bloody Could.' Indeed, on that first day of all, had not the guns of the Indian naval ships, in a brief euphoric moment of mutiny, been trained on the Bombay waterfront, even on the sacred Yacht Club itself? It all seemed a very long time ago.

Not only India had changed. I had changed; everything had changed.

*

At the airline counter they had never heard of us nor our hotel reservation; we brandished the certified copy of London office's telegram before their sleepy eyes but they knew nothing; the confirmed booking had not been made, the hotel had not been advised; they were regretting. The officials fidgeted vaguely, anxious to dispose of other people's dilemma; they withdrew into a reverie; already we had been forgotten.

Once again I felt the sense of useless mystery : what *does* happen to telegrams in India ? In many years I can remember hardly one arriving on time, or at the right place, or finding itself in the right hands. Ours had been four days on the way; it had not arrived, or perhaps it had arrived long ago and lay forgotten in somebody's in-tray, where it would rest forever. I loitered fretfully at the counter, waiting as one always does for the inspirational phrase that will convey despair without passion; they looked back at us with patient, courteous indifference, hoping we would go away. They had all the time in the world and we had not; they could afford to wait.

In this situation India will always win. There is no purpose in being right if one is powerless. To give way to anger is to surrender. It was not after all their fault.

'Could you perhaps very kindly help us ?'

Ruefully yet tolerantly the official reached for the phone and dialled a couple of numbers. The second one appeared to work.

'Hillcrest Hotel, two nights. Is not being Three-Star Taj, you understand. Moderate. Clean.'

'We're deeply obliged.' As always relief and exhaustion dissolved into effusive gratitude.

'Don't mention.' One problem was solved, now perhaps we would go away.

The taxi drove us through the damp dawn. Wherever Hillcrest might be it lay well outside the mainstream of downtown Bombay. We seem to be at once in the suburban wastelands, neither city nor country, a tattered region of

13

half-built housing and power-lines and billboards beside
a slovenly watercourse, just beginning to flicker its reflec-
tion of the rising sun. It was still not yet six o'clock, but
the desolate place was already awake. In India as in China,
as all over Asia, it is never too early to be ahead of the
plodding figures on the road, the tiny wickerwork stalls
preparing for business.

On the empty scrub by the roadside and along the creek
were half a dozen squatting figures, concerned with the
morning evacuation of their bowels. In half a mile they
had become a score, and then hundreds; the further we
drove the longer and more densely packed were the lines
of citizens on their haunches, dhotis gathered up, rapt and
concentrated on the pleasurable business of defecation. It
would appear that the urge had come simultaneously to
the whole suburban population. Very soon the line of
squatters had dragged out for miles, as though assembled
to watch some parade. For some it would seem to be a
convenient occasion for meditation, or even for forty winks;
for others this great communal shitting-time was clearly
a social activity, they shuffled sideways to approach one
another, chattering and waving limp fingers. It is true they
faced the roadway; the spectacle would otherwise have
been perhaps even more disturbing.

It is an enduring mystery why the Municipality – or the
Tourist Board, or the airline, or whoever occupies himself with these matters – so ordains it that multitudes of
visitors and strangers should be introduced to the country
in this way, to find that the Gateway to India is a public
shithouse many miles long – or, if they are unlucky enough
to ride by when the hour has passed, an avenue of small
heaps of faeces. One would not have to be especially fas-
tidious to feel that this, as a public-relations gesture, is
whimsical indeed.

V. S. Naipaul deeply outraged the Indian Establishment

by the strictures and comments in his book *An Area of Darkness*, but probably most of all by his obsessive distaste with the Indians' carefree attitude to the emptying of their entrails. 'Indians defecate everywhere. They defecate, mostly, by the railway tracks. But they also defecate on the beaches; they defecate on the hills; they defecate by the river banks; they defecate on the streets; they never look for cover. Muslims, with their tradition of purdah, can be at times secretive. But this is a religious act of self-denial, for it is said that the peasant, Muslim or Hindu, suffers from claustrophobia if he has to use an enclosed latrine....'

V. S. Naipaul gave much consideration to this phenomenon, as indeed it is difficult not to do to something the evidence of which is so pervasive. He remarks that the squatting Indian, who to the foreigner is an almost emblematic figure, is never publicly commented upon, never featured in novels or essays, never appears in the most 'realistic' documentary Indian cinema. He argues that this might be due to the intellectuals' permissible delicacy, analogous in some obscure way to the film-censor's revulsion at the act of kissing. But he knows that this is not true, and that the fact is that to an Indian the squatters are technically invisible. He can even deny their existence, with the limpid sincerity an Indian invokes when he is cosmically kidding himself. His rationalisation is that the Hindus' dread of pollution makes them the personally cleanest people in the world. The paradox is that this is in its own way perfectly true. Hindu custom requires an obligatory daily bath, and I have never been anywhere in India where it is not manifestly obeyed; in the most wretched and abominable quarters of the city dawn finds the hungry derelicts and street-sleepers lining up at the stand-pipe for the meticulous body-wash ritual. An Indian man or woman has to be lowly indeed not to wear fresh-laundered cotton on the body; however exiguous and worn the dhoti or sari may be, it is rarely soiled. Yet Indians of all varieties from the plump immaculate babu to the elegant housewife slumming in the bazaar will promenade through streets of almost indescribable filth and neglect, littered with refuse and debris, gutters adrift with ordure, picking their way through the muck with a skilfully intuitive indifference, since *they do not see it*. Themselves in their persons they are clean, all else is *maya*, or illusion. Daily life is governed by complex rules to insulate themselves from ritual contamination – the right hand alone is used for feeding, the left reserved for impure or ignoble purposes; the methodology of defecation is laid down, therefore where it takes place is of no consequence. Actually to observe the roadside squatters, and worse to remark on them, is to be both offensive and superficial, since it perceives the surface and not the substance. There comes a point where the most courteous of Indians will lose patience with this sort of pedantry and sharply remind one of the more disgusting manners of the West – the employment of the right hand in sex and slops, the repellent use of toilet-paper, the bathing in tub-water sullied by the body's dirt. As they recount these murky habits their eyes clear and their smiles return: by criticising the West they are justifying the East; by and by the wayside excrement and the open sewers have slipped into forgetfulness, where they belong.

The Hillcrest Hotel was, as the airport man had foretold, clearly not the Taj. Hotels that will accept one without reservation at six in the morning rarely are. Its small pretentions – a canopy, an electric sign: 'Hi c est Hote', a chaukidar in a white jacket – were diminished by being at the end of an alley in which it was impossible to turn a car. After fourteen hours imprisoned in an aircraft from which for security reasons we had been unable to disembark at any staging-point, and at that godforsaken time in the morning, it was a godsend. We climbed up to an unidentifiable room, and slept until noon.

Indeed I had changed.

*

We took a hair-raising taxi ride into the city. The rush-hour traffic of Bombay is a nightmare — not from dementia, as in Tokyo, nor from exuberance, as in Rome; not from malice, as in Paris; it is a chaos rooted in years of practised confusion, absent-mindedness, selfishness, inertia, and an incomplete understanding of mechanics. There are no discernible rules. The little Fiat cabs are old, but not as old as they appear; a few years of the Bombay free-for-all have aged them beyond their years. Our taxi's bumpers were tied on with wire; the steering-wheel had a play of about fifty degrees. It also appeared to be firing on about one and a half cylinders, and the driver had difficulty in maintaining any revolutions. In consequence when he achieved any momentum he was reluctant to lose it, so that we would always swerve rather than brake, with a steady obligato on the horn.

Everything went too fast for safety, too slowly for speed. The pedestrians abounded, swarming like white butterflies in vague, suicidal trances, either in violent conversation or in a mindless reverie. A place of especial peril was the striped pedestrian crossing. On approaching one of these sanctuaries all drivers crowded on an extra spurt of speed and charged across, horns blaring. I have always had a real fear of travelling in Indian cars, nor you may be sure, after this last year, have I lost it now.

Downtown Bombay seemed transformed. For one thing

17

the city had changed its *shape*, physically. There was no longer an inch of room to spare for the erection of the concrete commercial rectangles that even the poorest societies feel obliged to display, so they were building in the sea. Long stretches of foreshore were being reclaimed; I was told in all seriousness that land was changing hands at the equivalent of a thousand pounds a *square foot*. This may have been hyperbole, but one can never afford to disbelieve anything in India.

In the city where ninety thousand people sleep at nights on the streets, expensive new apartment blocks were sprouting everywhere – they were called, with the Indian gift of almost knowing what words mean: 'Monolith', 'Acropolis 1, 2, and 3', 'Il Palazzo', or 'Flowerdene'.

I demanded to indulge my nostalgia and visit the Taj, the hotel that had not received our reservation. The Taj is, or was, a truly splendid institution, built on a properly ample and satisfying old-fashioned scale, with just enough schmaltzy opulence to suit my taste: vast public spaces, a huge and famous stairwell with open galleries round every floor, like a really four-star prison. I was rather taken aback to find that this grand place had sprouted an even more massive annexe on the skyscraper plan, to my mind gravely falsifying its character, like an aristocratic old lady in a sports car. But I delighted in the original, as I always had done. This had been my very first lodging in India, twenty-five years ago.

I had arrived, all those years past, under the guidance of an Old India Hand.

'And at the end of it all,' he had said to me, 'you will know less of the country than you do now. I take it that you would not have come to India without filling your head with some sort of nonsensical misinformation.'

I was in a mood to believe him. There is a moment, shortly after one's first arrival in India, when all one's preconceptions seem built on the most preposterous fallacies, when everything in sight undermines one's meagre stock of basic facts, when one bows meekly to the traditional cynicism of the Old Hand. I had indeed filled my head with a great deal. I had imagined it necessary to begin work among the wild intricacies of the Indian scene by fuelling up initially with book-lore and statistical porridge of all kinds. It had been far from dull work; even then India had appeared to me without parallel as a source of complex and rewarding extravagances in every political, social, religious aspect. I reckoned I knew something of the theory of this rich mass. And already I recognised the crude truth of what the Old Hand said : everything I saw suggested something more the books had failed to mention.

The Taj had received me glumly; even then the pattern was well established and my cable had gone astray. The hotel was wholly booked, they told me, the coming jubilee of the Aga Khan and the impending ceremony of weighing him in diamonds had crammed the place with customers a good deal more useful than I had the appearance of being.

I was shown into a vast room with six narrow beds in rows, like a cottage hospital. My two very small bags were brought up and the six drooping coolies who had co-operated in carrying them formed up in attitudes of classic humility and hope. I distributed the coins in my pocket; instantly the submissiveness disappeared and a burst of furious argument arose, the porters abandoned me and formed a protest meeting around one of their number who had apparently come in for two annas more than his share. I suggested that they continue their accountancy outside while I changed my clothes; they paid not the slightest heed, but wrangled more shrilly than ever.

Halfway through the performance one of my room-mates entered, a heavy man in a canvas hat. He regarded the scene with disfavour, and boomed 'Fuck off!' in a powerful voice, at which the entire company vanished with the utmost alacrity.

'Worth learning a few useful phrases,' he said.

Those were the days of the Taj's penultimate and merry heyday, with the fading Raj symbolically crowding the marble halls in a revelry of uniforms and blond moustaches, knowing that things would never be again as they were now.

After half an hour's interlude for nostalgia, Moni and I went out together to take possession of Bombay. I had been everywhere, in every kind of circumstance, but I had never been anywhere before with a partner. In all my hesitant and fumbling explorations of the world before I had always been alone; solitude and alienation had become a formula to which one adjusted with diminishing regret. Now that quality of loneliness had gone. I felt an unreasonable elation, as though I had somehow emerged from probation.

Outside the Taj there was a boy with an armful of instruments for sale: a kind of two-stringed fiddle based on the resonance of a coconut-shell. He was playing a vague air in a minor key that I would have sworn was a Hebrew folk-tune. He smiled broadly; I wanted to give him a coin to express the incongruity of my surprise, but astonishingly he did not want it; he was not begging, he was selling fiddles.

Bombay is a discouraging aspect of India, but on that first day – or was it the fifty-first? – I could not have enough of it. Its main open space is dominated by a vast line of University buildings; our heritage. The brazen sun beat down upon them from a blazing sky. Brown students swarmed in and out in Asian clothes. Yet the English had chosen to build this University in Bombay in a style of the most fearsome Victorian Gothic Revival, a red pile of gables and pointed arches and finials and whatnot; in the country that had made the brilliance of the Madurai temple and had absorbed alien elegance of the Taj Mahal they laboured and brought forth something like a Prudential Building, or a Huddersfield Town Hall. It was a gesture not necessarily arrogant or even patronising; it was just another example of how the Raj in the day of its dominance could be so effortlessly and mindlessly wrong. They were wrong when they built this Victorian Gothic extravagance in Bombay only because it was blindly perverse. They could be equally wrong when they chose to isolate themselves symbolically from the Hindu life-style by adopting unerringly its most unpleasant aspect: the caste system. Caste Hindus followed the disagreeable rule of refusing to eat with anyone outside their own social-religious group; exactly so did the English rulers. If Hindus invented caste, the English invented the Club. Clubs were everywhere, but here in Bombay was a notorious example, the Yacht Club. When I first saw Bombay no Indian could be a guest there, let alone a member. Thus the Raj paid its respects to the most insulting custom of the society it affected to despise, and created Anglo-Saxon Brahminism, the one thing that will never be forgotten. It would have been no less preposterous, and maybe made more sense, had they declared it necessary for their own memsahibs to have set themselves afire on their husband's graves.

Similarly in Bombay there was a great patchwork of ethnic patterns – Marathas, Gujeratis, Goans, and so on, with a rich variety of faiths: Hindus, Muslims, Jains. Any of them could have been selected as official pets. But no: the English eccentrically chose the one sect that was not even Indian: the Parsis. The Parsis were refugees from Persia, they observed the obscure and somewhat distasteful customs of Zoroastrianism, such as exposing their dead on platforms to be torn up and devoured by the vultures. These non-Indians – perhaps because they *were* non-Indian – the English adopted as their favourite sons, and greatly did the Parsi community prosper thereby.

All this seemed of singularly little importance to either Moni or me as we plodded round this hideously exciting city. We came upon a piece of parkland where a small group had gathered around a man who had planted himself upside-down in the ground. He had dug a small hole into which he had buried his head and neck and packed the red soil around them; the rest of his thin body stood vertically up from the ground like a rooted sapling : he had clearly deprived himself of air or breath, he had reversed not only himself but nature, and there he stayed. It seemed an extraordinary easy way to make a living, if that was his intention; whether passers-by dropped coins around him or not he could never know, since he had chosen the most inarticulate form of demonstration possible. If it were a trick it was clearly ingenious far beyond the hope of reward; if it were a penance, why the bowl for alms beside his buried head? I was full of curiosity : how long could he possibly stay there in this intricate denial of reality? It might be days, said Moni; they find oxygen in the ground. I argued that this was impossible, it was one of our doctrinal differences never to be resolved.

On the open space had been set up a big marquee with placards and billboards all around : 'HAIL AND HOMAGE TO HIS DIVINE GRACE GURU SOMETHING-JI.' *His Divine Grace?* Who could this swami be, who claimed both the divinity and grace that neither Gandhi nor the Buddha ever dared do? There were now so many of them : nondescript bearded swamis or obese and epicene boys, ostentatiously unpleasant frauds freeloading on youth's despair; they had timely turned the tables on the West. The park was full of baby Americans. Scores of them sat mournfully around,

shaven skulls with the *choti* tuft over pallid undernour-
ished faces the colour of Parmesan cheese; from time to
time they shuffled round in a sort of clumsy conga-line,
clinking small cymbals: 'Hare Krishna, Ram Ram, Hare
Ram.' They were to be found in London's Oxford Street,
in Munich, in Amsterdam, in Chicago; in these places
they had a kind of challenging pathos, a sort of desperation; in India they made my compassion curdle. I had one
of many arguments with Moni about these bloodless refugees impersonating an easy ideal. I became angry and
blimpish: I said that this charade debases the culture it
affects to reveal. I insisted that they had every right to
reject their own social pattern, but not to corrupt another.

My wife with her inexhaustible Hindu tolerance said:
they do no harm. My nonconformist impatience vigorously
disagreed. Her reproof laid the finger precisely upon my
irritation: what had I got against these inane white kids
aping India, turning their silly reverence into a parody?
Because I was here before, and saw it sooner? Because their
naïveté was both bogus and genuine, stupid and crafty?
Because I was jealous of any sort of faith, even this vapid
kind?

This I might just have believed, until I found in Mere-
weather Street another blond bearded American paleface
in unclean khaddar cloth on the pavement behind a
begging-bowl and a card: 'I am hungry.' I was outraged
into a neo-colonial exasperation: an able-bodied member
of the richest society on earth sponging on the poorest.

'What's the idea?'

'Hare Krishna, brother.'

'Hare Ram, Nitai Gaura Radheshyam to you. What's
the rest of the mantra?'

'Hare Krishna, brother.'

'Yanks go home.' I stump off righteously. A group of
Indians pause, surprised at my bad manners.

'Perhaps,' says Moni, 'he was hungry.'

'Nonsense; he was full of *bhanga*. That's why he came.'

'You never know,' says my wife. I am exasperated beyond measure at her tolerance and puff up like a sahib.

'One more beggar,' she says, 'in a country of beggars.'

3

In the year to come, after the long trauma of illness, I was to look back on this period with a kind of affectionate dismay. I was in the throes of what Simone Weil, in her tragic and tormented wartime exile among the English, called 'The Need for Roots'. Certainly this *enracinement* of her meaning had eluded me most of my life, but I supposed this to be the result less of some temperamental disadvantage in me than of all manner of random hazards: my father's whimsical attempts, after the disintegration of our home, to establish us in the cheap economy of Europe between the wars, my own dependence on a vagrant life – first by choice, then from necessity. I can recall making hardly any really conscious choice of any development in my life; clearly I was attended more by good luck than good intention.

However, a choice of some moment had been made now. I was going south to meet my new family for the first time.

Only once before had I ever been to the city of Bangalore. In those days it had been part of the State of Mysore, a princely fiefdom that theoretically was still an autocracy of the most mediaeval kind, but whose enlightened Government had achieved a form of social progress that left most of British India far behind. I was then still nevertheless a peripheral part of the Raj and there were certain accepted courtesies; the Maharaja's Government had hospitably sent to look after me a dapper and forthcoming young official called Sri Srivasan.

'The "Sri", as you know, is customarily an honorific. In my case not so, is being merely my name. As your better-class Americans will, I am told, use the name of "Earl", and indeed sometimes "Duke".'

He was the most able and agreeable of cicerones. No young man could have been more elegant in his dress, which was strictly European – almost Central European, down to lavender suits and parti-coloured shoes. He was indefatigable, intelligent and resourceful. He took me to see the porcelain factory, the sandalwood-soap factory, and the Lunatic Asylum. Then he took me to see the Fort, and the Gardens of Hyder Ali, and the Sewage Disposal, and the cave temple of Gangadhareswara, with the emblems of Shiva – the Trident, the Umbrella, the Double Drum – monumentally carved from solid masonry. Farther yet, to temples enscrolled and turbulent with tormented stone, emblazoned with holy erotica, the *lingam* and the *yoni*, the worshipful fundament, the formalised *maithuna* embraces, vast and elaborate phalli, canonised flesh, the goddess Yanhuma on the tortoise, Vishnu enfolded in the coils of the Eternity-Serpent, everywhere an apotheosis of the magical lust. It was all a great change from the pine-wood austerities of my late grandfather's Free Kirk in Pollokshields.

Here Sri Sri became eloquent and illuminating; he spoke with a curious objectivity of his violent South Indian Hinduism, or perhaps Hinduistic Indianism; the matter of the difference is excruciatingly complex. There were moments in my early exposure to it when I was persuaded that it was gracious rather than cruel, poetic rather than barbarous, colourful rather than crude. Dissociated firmly from its sociological context it had the intricate permutations of some strangely satisfying algebraic formula, and

26

to me equally incomprehensible.

The outward manifestations had a weird insistence, a laboriously joyful complication of imagery and execution that in those early days of wonder I found hypnotic – no line, no bas-relief panels and friezes but capitals and architraves in supersensual relief, incised and rounded by cutting deeply enough to encompass the depth of the image, tortured and restless, presenting every emotion but one: peace.

The temples abounded. In the morning we would pass drifting lines of women bound for the Uprising formula, when the god would be taken from bed, washed and anointed and seated for the day; they carried brass cruets with the holders for sandalwood-powder, ghee, curds and rice, in the other hand a jasmine chaplet. They pattered into the dark entrances chattering and shrilling. Hindu temples are not temples in any other sense than being simple shrines, a dwelling for the image of the godling, collecting-houses for tithes; a good Hindu need never attend them for worship, for the word has no real application. He has no ritual necessity to realise symbolically his union to his god or his faith, or however he would define it (which of course he can never do); to the Hindu this fact is basic; he is of those who are programmed to discern within themselves an expression of endlessness; it is fundamentally established that he is something that, in the final sequence of interrupted births, will return to whence he came, which is nowhere. The treatment of the deity in the shrine is therefore a simple matter of tending the image as though it were a creature and ordering the routine of its days. He will agree that this, like all else, is *maya*, which is illusion, that reality lies far elsewhere, yet fundamentally even he could yet inlay his life-style with a maddening pattern of sanctions and formulae, of devices of propitiation to contain permutations among thirty thousand sub-deities which, if correctly performed, could occupy his entire life. Even then such an impeccable product as Sri could wear his talisman beneath his sharp lavender suit, his *zonar*, symbolic thread of Brahminical second-birth, could feel himself obliged to leave his portable radio and bathe himself with the prescribed mixture of the Four Gifts: the milk, the ghee, the curds and the cow-dung, the food of the gods.

Other peoples may have shared particular faiths, beliefs, convictions, superstitions or whatever they may be, but India is Hinduism and Hinduism is India. The exigencies of modern politics have tried very hard to obscure this, but it is ineluctable. The Arab lands are Muslim, but there are many Muslim lands. The Mediterranean is Catholic, but there are many Catholic peoples. There is no Hindu nation but India, there never was and there never can be. The existence of an enormous minority of sixty million or so Indian Muslims, the biggest in the world, makes no difference at all to this categorical imperative, however troublesome it may be to the desperate Indian reformists and modernists who would make the nation what its Constitution enjoins, a secular state. It *is* a secular state; yet it is inescapably Hindu and, I dare say, will always be, since Hinduism has the unsought faculty of absorbing and digesting every kind of intrusion. This is of course simply because it is not a *persuasion*, it is not an activity, it is not even a spiritual methodology; Hinduism is flesh of India's flesh and bone of her bone, proclaimed unnoticed in every perceptible function of life: the sacred yet starving cattle wandering with their certain immunity among the furious traffic of Calcutta, the endless ablutions among the garbage, the acceptances and the submissions, the voiceless inequalities, the sudden bursts of barbaric beauty: all this has nothing to do with faith, since it is the inescapable fabric of existence, at the

28

same time its foundation and its destruction.

Ever since the early Indian days I have found it hard to argue myself out of this useless enchantment with the superficialities of Hinduism – myself, I suppose, by any colloquial standards an atheist, or more likely a sentimental sceptic, heavily infected by the customary doubts and dreads of the materialist. Why should the end-product of generations of Scottish heathen-haters feel any kinship with this obsessive fantasy? Almost certainly through the meanest of qualities, which is curiosity.

'Tolerance,' wrote Gandhi – an agreeable, meaningless word – 'implies a gratuitous assumption of other faiths to one's own, whereas *ahimsa* teaches us to entertain for the faiths of others the same respect as we accord our own, thus admitting the imperfections of the latter.'

But if there is no 'latter' in the meaning the man intended? I would have asked these questions of Sri, but he was busy, determining the effects of petrol-rationing on the further use of the State car.

*

In those days I had been a newspaper correspondent making what freshman sense I could make of this mosaic of a country I barely knew. There had been everything to gain and nothing to lose in personal relationship, since I had none. This time, this occasion, was very different and much more momentous: I was going to be presented to my wife's family for the first time. No man can face this situation without uneasiness, and these circumstances were exceptional. As far as either Moni or I knew no European had joined the family before. Nor had I even applied for admittance; I had endured no probationary period, I had entered the door without knocking, the parents had been informed by letter. Even I was compelled to feel that the whole thing was a stupendous sort of impertinence. I had, everyone knew, little enough to commend me; I had no money, no property, no distinction of family. It was true that Moni was somewhat too mature and experienced to qualify for an arranged marriage on the Indian economic or dynastic principle; this was as well for me, since by neither standard could I have been considered much of a candidate. However, the thing was done, and by now meant so much to me that its family endorsement just had to be successful.

From the first moment it was abundantly successful. Father and Mother were there to meet us; he wore his best suit and she a pale sari; in their seventies they were handsome people in my eyes. They were also clearly as nervous as I. Within a moment it was clear without explanation that all would be well.

My parents-in-law's name was Appachoo. However, the system of names in South India is extremely intricate; indeed I never came properly to master it. 'Appachoo' was my father-in-law's given name, peculiar to him. His first name, which was Kandrathandar, was his family name. His second name, Ayappa, was his father's given name. He, however, came from a very small and tribal state with a clan tradition almost exactly akin to that of the Scottish Highlands, where the family name was of great significance. In Mysore and Madras, however, a man's first name defined not his family but his place of origin. Inevitably, and to prevent themselves going mad, South Indians tend to call themselves merely by their first initials: my father-in-law was 'K.A.' But equally inevitably, given this methodology, all his brothers must be called 'K.A.' It was as well that all South Indians are reputed to have prodigious memories.

It added to the newcomer's difficulties that in no circumstances will any South Indian wife *say aloud* her husband's name, for deeply obscure and ironclad traditional reasons. When addressing him she will use all manner of oblique phrases: 'Look here', 'I say there', 'Hello'. When referring to him she will say 'my husband' but never articulate his name. My wife Moni told me that she knew married friends whom she had tried by every sort of trick and stratagem to entrap into speaking their husband's names; for twenty years she had never once succeeded.

With my own in-laws there was no problem; he was 'Aja' and she was 'Mamma'.

There is also the factor, alarming to many, that when you marry into an Indian family you abruptly acquire a daunting number of relatives. Indian families not only embrace all the available generations in a mutual unity of dependence, the definition of relative extends like the circles of a pebble dropped in a pool, to cousins, aunts, second cousins twice removed, and all the ancillary relationships *they* have accumulated through marriage, farther and farther out until the bonds of consanguinity are barely discernible at all. A European husband may well find himself with a new kinship half-a-dozen strong; an Indian one must come to terms with an uncountable regiment of relations, more of whom continually appear, recede, and reappear. He must accustom himself to being greeted tenderly by the sweet and nubile daughters of his wife's third cousin, and called 'Uncle', the all-purpose Indian honorific for all men even marginally older than themselves. Above all, he must adjust to the dawning knowledge that of this multifarious and assorted clan every member, however remote, will be continually and minutely informed of every detail of the private life and circumstances of every other one.

Greater complications could appear. There was Moni's brother-in-law, Baba, husband of her sister. His grandparents had had three daughters, but no son; he was the child of one of the daughters. It was necessary for the grandfather somehow to acquire a male heir, for reasons of dignity, inheritance, and to perform the obligatory Hindu rites at his death. In India, the customary solution for this difficulty is adoption. So the grandfather adopted Baba. Baba therefore became legally his grandfather's son, and in consequence his own mother's brother. It seemed in no way to disturb their poise.

I used to love walking about. When Moni was involved in family occasions I plodded around Bangalore. It is not a distinguished nor especially attractive city, but it is both vastly expanding and gloomily haunted. The total possession of India by the British – dissolving so rapidly elsewhere, leaving behind its tidewrack of conflicting cultures, of imitative clothing and manners, of a language imperfectly mastered, of Victorian official formulae – had somehow clung to Bangalore. The place was haunted not just by the Raj but by the Army of the Raj. It had been a great military establishment; it was no longer, and yet the ghosts remained. This big industrial, engineering, aeroplane-making city of a million independent Indians still divided itself into Civil Lines, Cantonment, bazaar. Statues of Victoria and Edward still stood untouched, probably the last in India. The street names still remained: Cavalry Road, Garrison Road, Brigade Road. Christian churches abounded – missions, bible societies, evangelicals, Pentecostals. What could be the nature of a Pentecostal South Indian?

I went into a coffee-shop; inside were a handful of very old Anglo-Indian survivors, dressed in khaki-drill and the sola topis of a vanished age. The café had made the mistake of printing a quotation from Ruskin on its plastic-covered bill of fare. 'Quality is never the result of an accident. It is always the result of intelligent effort. There must be the will to produce a superior thing.' The thick

32

white cup was cracked, the coffee was cold. This was the permanent Indian confusion of the symbol with the fact. Because someone had discovered Ruskin's words, his principle was obviously fulfilled. 'There must be the will to produce a superior thing.' Should not there also be the ability, or even the intention, to do so? This was not necessary: having proclaimed the truism, that was enough.

I went into a bookshop. The shelves were full mostly of technical works or expensive guide-books. Wherever I went the attendant moved and stood behind me watchfully, never taking his eyes from me. If I moved but a yard, he moved a yard. He literally breathed down my neck. Did he suspect me of shoplifting? Was he a critic appraising my choice? For ten minutes I felt him at my shoulder.

Finally: 'If you stand watching me I can't concentrate.'

He gave no reply.

'You are making me uneasy.'

'Yes, sir.'

'Please leave me alone for a few minutes.'

He did not move.

After some more minutes of this I said: 'I'll just have to go.'

'Yes, sir. You want buy a book?'

A small excitement breathed over the street outside: the President was driving by; he was visiting Bangalore, and his cavalcade was just three cars. Here and there passers-by waved and made *namaskar*; the old gentleman saluted absently. I recalled things being otherwise: in the Ghana of Nkrumah's day, whenever the Redeemer passed police outriders made everyone get out of their cars ten minutes before. There had been occupied Tokyo – each time General MacArthur arrived at or left his Dai Ichi Building the whole city came to a standstill; it was like the Second Coming twice a day. In Bangalore nobody bothered much about old Giri. Prime Ministers are one thing,

Presidents are another. Who knows the name of the President of Cuba? Or, for that matter, of the Soviet Union?

Later Aja was to take me to his club, the institute, which had always been Indian. The barman apologetically refused to serve us – I was not wearing Proper Shoes. On my feet were sandals. I was in fact wearing the Indian chapals I, like most people, always wore; now they counted as improper dress.

My route took me past a place where a small man was splitting a single enormous log, with iron wedges. Each time I passed the log grew smaller. As the days went by it grew smaller and smaller, until it was reduced to firewood.

There is much to be said for retaining the past. I suppose I am at heart, in everything but politics, a rooted conservative. Our quarters in the West End Hotel were what I happily remembered of the old Indian hotels of long ago – a compound with sprawling great rooms scattered far apart, ticking fans, vast *almirahs*, which are wardrobes, with heavy brass fittings, beds with posts, gloom inside, and past the verandah a spread of lawns, a burst of flame-trees as though the garden was afire. It will be a sad day when these great Edwardian hotel-compounds full of space and distance, probably wholly uneconomic, give place to the tall town-type put-you-up chainstores that now litter the world with their expensively boring vulgarity.

Almost every day Aja would come round with a gift of fruit. He had long ago retired, he and Mama lived in a small cool house with a most wonderful garden. When they had come to the house twenty years ago it had been set in a compound that had gone to jungle. It was now immaculate, nurtured and cherished, like a tiny Botanical Garden. All Aja's concentrated love was focused on this compound, which now produced in abundance at least

34

fourteen different fruits, all growing exuberantly out of a compressed reddish soil that looked about as fertile as a hard tennis-court. There grew papaya, pomegranate, mulberry, limes, grapes, cardomom, pomelo and guava, avocado which here is called Butterfruit, at least three varieties of mango – malgoa, nilambi, bangaanpali, each more delicious than the other – custard-apple, bull's-heart, plantain; a jackfruit tree with its enormous green fruit, weird objects the size of footballs with delicately patterned rind like a reptile's skin; little brown chukus that look like cocoa-covered golf-balls and taste like fibrous honey with a glossy stone like polished ebony. There were the quaint little rose-apples, that to begin with taste of nothing at all until you realise you are eating the *scent* of roses....

Since his accident Aja had walked with some difficulty, but he spent much of his time circling slowly round his vegetable family, on the most intimate terms not only with every tree and bush (had he not reared each and every one from a sapling or a seed?) but, it sometimes seemed, every individual fruit, knowing exactly to a day the appointed moment of its apotheosis. 'That jack will be ready by Tuesday afternoon, round about five. In three days I shall have sixteen nice rose-apples for you.'

They grew their own coffee. The Government required that all coffee-plantations of more than twenty trees must be registered, so they took care to grow exactly nineteen. Their coffee – grown themselves, cured themselves, roasted and ground within twenty feet of the berries' birthplace – was better than anything I ever tasted in the region, and really good South Indian coffee is incomparably the best, just as the bogus coffee to be found in Delhi and the north is unchallengeably the worst.

There was even a miniature vineyard, on pergolas of concrete poles, from which Mama made her own wine. It was not wholly to my taste, resembling as it did a peculiar

35

form of curried Dubonnet; it was powerfully fruity and sweet and could have passed for a very eccentric port, with the very deceptive nursery-taste of country wine. My brother-in-law would sometimes encourage it with a dash or two of Carew's gin, when it would quite swiftly become very festive indeed.

But transcending all other of Mama's loves and obsessions was her wonderful motor-car. This was, and I hope still is, one of the grandeurs of Bangalore. It had been built by Morris in England in 1942, and in the twenty-odd years that it had been an integral part of my in-laws' household – more, their family – it had been maintained and cherished with a dedication that verged on the sacramental. In the India of today the possession or acquisition of a car of any kind is a matter of much ingenuity, cunning, and expense. Aja and Mama had clung to their beautiful old banger not wholly out of sentiment.

The car was an object of great distinction, a period-piece with a highly developed functional role. It had been designed in the stumpy, four-square and no-nonsense fashion of thirty years ago; its outline was that which a child will produce when symbolising the word 'car'. Equally those had been the days when motor-cars were built to endure, and endure is what Mama's Morris had done; you could almost feel in its squat self-confidence its own appreciation of its years, and its tender attention in the garage which was more like an intensive-care unit. It wore its original paintwork, grey and glossy and immaculate; its middle-aged engine, settled in its ways, turned over at a touch with a comfortable steadfast clunk – as well it might, since at the hint of a wheeze or a knock Mama's mechanic would be round, himself a decade younger than the car, who had grown up on the care and treatment of its speckless moving parts. Together he and Mama would undress it, rub it with unguents, croon over it, put it into shape. It never went wrong, because it never had a chance. It had trundled round the city while Bangalore grew from a provincial backwater into a great sprawling industrial city, and its stately chunter through the flame-tree avenues was a daily decoration to the scene. There was a rule that it should never be driven after six in the evening, since the street lighting of Bangalore is sepulchral and deceptive, and there was always the peril of an encounter with a lunatic autoricksha or a contemplative cow. So the motor-car went to bed at sundown. I sometimes had the impression that Mama would arise at intervals in the night to tuck it in.

Between the orchard, the car, and each other, my parents-in-law contrived a life that was small and settled and serene. Our intrusion was accepted with happiness. It seemed to me evident from the first that we would get on together; I was nevertheless immeasurably relieved and heartened to discover that I was admitted with an instant affection that had as far as I could see no qualifications at all; from the first day that we walked about the little compound together and shared our first food in the little house I was clearly taken into the inner ring of an Indian family of which (as I was soon to discover) the expanding concentric circles went on pretty well forever. It was a very primitive lesson in the humanities, and I was foolish to have expected anything else; they loved their daughter, their daughter loved me, therefore they loved me. To be sure, Mama and Aja were of a strongly Anglophile tradition; I might have been less acceptable had I been a Hottentot or a Zulu, or at least in that case I would not have started off the odds-on favourite I happened to be. Yet I had little to commend me as a person but a certain adaptability, a familiarity with Indian custom and courtesy – I fulfilled no other of a good in-law's requirements, being both middle-aged and very far from well-off. At my time

37

of life a man marries with either financial resources or prospects, of which I conspicuously had neither. It is to Aja and Mama's eternal credit that at no time was the slightest reference made to this. (Doubtless the research had been done earlier, in which case the more greatly did I come to respect them.) After a couple of days I understood perfectly well that their home in Richards Town could at any time be our home, and that I admit is a feeling I have rarely had elsewhere.

In the mornings I would try to work. I would have liked to sit in the sun, but Indian rooms are designed, sensibly, to exclude every ray of sun that can be excluded. If I dragged my heavy chair out to the patch of dusty green that passed for a lawn – brittle discouraged green whiskers wilting on the red grit – I was distracted by the masons chipping away at bits of brick; they had been at the same changeless and apparently wholly unproductive task ever since we arrived; even the bricks seemed to be the same every day, and nothing emerged from this laconic work except scraping sounds and endless murmured argument. I tried in a desul-tory way to imagine what could be the possible end-purpose of this occupation. One of the men I took to be a foreman of sorts; he alone chipped nothing, but leaned against a tree smoking bidis and snapping reproofs at random. I asked him what was the nature of this undertaking; he said: 'Making with brick.'

When I sat in the sun people looked at me curiously: mad dogs and Englishmen, I thought, though I am no Englishman and it wanted three hours to noon. And of course they were right; four minutes in the open air turned the shirt into a dishrag, the sweat ran down the arms and soaked the writing-pad. I could take my shirt off, but that would be thought eccentric, if not scandalous. I could most probably drop my pants and leave a turd against a tree without causing comment, but to expose my meagre rib-cage to passers-by would have been unseemly. So I did the sensible thing and went back to the tiled shade of the verandah and tried to bend my mind to – alas, to anything; the putting-down of twenty consecutive words these days were like a treadmill; my brain grew duller every day.

The family on the next verandah were also taking the air; the women conversed together with great animation and all at once, like spiteful budgerigars. Why is it that any discourse between Indian ladies, however familial and doubtless affectionate, as they surely must be to live so closely packed together, must always sound peevish, rancorous, disputatious? It cannot be as with the Chinese, whose meaning itself is dependent on vocal pitch and where a love-call can sound like an imprecation. Tamil is not a tonal language, as far as I know. Yet when I come to think of it I cannot after all these years recall hearing a conversation between Indians that by its sound alone suggested tenderness. Always to the stranger's ear it has the strident overtone of argument. Only my wife seems capable of the gentler and reasonable modulations; maybe that is why she has such a job making herself understood to anyone but me.

By and by the neighbours tired of their seminar and turned on the transistor, we now got Madrasi film-music from Radio Ceylon, which everybody liked because it was a commercial station and its film-music was therefore especially pop and penetrating. It drove me mad, so I retreated still further, into the bedroom, which was sub-limely cool but so dark I could not even attempt to work, thank God.

At this point the processions began. The first knock on the door was not really a knock, more of a diffident scratch, a hint that someone was trying without any real assurance

39

to make his presence known. This was the food-bearer come for the breakfast things; he would take away the coffee-pot and a cup. Soon he would be back to collect the plate, a knife and a fork. A reasonable interval would elapse before he returned for the honey, and later for the napkins. His final appearance would be to examine the table for any items overlooked on the previous trips; this would be rewarded by the discovery of a single teaspoon on the desk. I had been saving it up for my afternoon mango, but it could not be suffered to remain.

South Indian domestic servants are grand masters at the art of fiddling about, which is to say of achieving the absolute minimum of accomplishment through the expenditure of the most conspicuous activity. I have seen a bearer swab a table all the way round a single pencil left lying there. This is clearly more difficult and time-consuming than lifting up the pencil, but it also implies greater assiduity and consideration: if the master wants the pencil exactly there, so be it, the few square inches of dust it conceals will be his responsibility, not mine.

Five minutes would now elapse before the next visitation; this was the room-bearer enquiring about my laundry. It was ready there in the corner, but I had forgotten to make out the dhobi-list. I must now go through the form for the appropriate ticks – bedsheets, blouses, banians, dhotis silk and dhotis cotton, underpants long and ditto short, saris silk and georgette, woollen jerseys (for God's sake who wears woollen jerseys in Bangalore?) and, at last, shirts and socks, Per Each.

The dhobi-wallah dematerialised; in descending order he was replaced in the doorway by the wavering khaki figure of the room-sweeper, craving the privilege of entering to flap his cloth with a dedicated lack of purpose around the floor, his attitude simultaneously absent yet anxious, his role to achieve invisibility as befitted his station in life and yet to demonstrate enough small fuss to justify his job: a delicate duality. He must be abased and silent, yet somehow evident, careful never to raise his eyes, squatting crabwise about the room among the dust which is his livelihood and which therefore must be identified with, stirred and agitated and shifted from one place to another. He was a sweeper, and his function therefore to *be* a sweeper, not necessarily effectively to sweep. He fulfilled the role society required of him merely by associating himself as nearly as he could with the dirt in which he dealt; his efficiency was of minor importance. A vacuum cleaner would work better, but it would cost more.

One would think that by now the end had been reached, the ritual accomplished, but not so; there was yet one more shadow to salaam and he hesitated in the doorway with even greater self-deprecation: it was the turn of the bathroom-sweeper to creep across the tiles with his rag and his tin can of disinfectant, to propel the shallow pools of water from the defective wastepipe about the floor and distribute them so that they might more readily evaporate.

In India the educated may do many things, run many businesses, diversify and prosper, but the baser workers are specialists of the most precise and narrow kind; the more menial the task the more exclusive its nature. A room-bearer can carry a flask of water but not a cup of tea; a floor-sweeper can make the cigarette-ash float up and subside, but he will not clean toilets. The rules govern everything, of custom and caste and routine and rote; to each his appointedly small hierarchical place in the system, as it was in the beginning and ever more shall be. Thus every operation however simple and elementary will be divided and subdivided into a multiplicity of activities, each one so trifling that it cannot in reason ask a living wage, requiring at the very bottom little but the performance, or role, of servility, to be seen in manifest lowliness, to be ever present on the floor or in the shadows to remind its betters at all times that an established society admits always of one step lower. This is *dharma*, the inescapable duty that is the core of Hinduism itself – *dharma*, the distillation of virtue and hope for the reward of a better life after death in the endless cycle of rebirth, the total acceptance of a condition whatever it may be, total conformity with the laws of behaviour that condition enjoins, and the lower that condition the greater metaphysical possibilities for its improvement. The fatalism of the poor in India is not apathy but dissociation from unhappiness, just as the cruel indifference of the rich around them is not necessarily callous, or cynical, but an equal acceptance of the *dharma* that feeds them and keeps the others hungry.

Hinduism – whatever Hinduism may be – is so vast, so elastic, so eclectic, so accommodating to the believers in one God, ten thousand gods, or no gods at all, embodying everything from the most elaborate envisionments of the Brahmin mind to a granite phallus in a cave, is yet held together by two primary concepts: *karma*, the reward or punishment in the next life for the behaviour in this; and *dharma*, the obligation to accept one's condition and perform the duties appropriate to it. This is intrinsic to the whole principle of caste. Not only every individual but every *thing* has this attribute. It is the *dharma* of the wind to blow, and that of the rain to fall; it is the *dharma* of a stone to be hard and a leaf to be soft. It is likewise the *dharma* of a Brahmin to be respected, and that of a sweeper to be despised. There is no getting away from it. The sacred Bhagavadgita, which cannot properly be questioned, says: 'Even should one's *dharma* seem to be mad, its performance brings blessing more than the assumption and pursuit of another's *dharma*.'

42

At the same time it is not wholly sufficient for the individual simply to follow his *dharma*, he must accept without ambition to change, he must regard his misfortune or otherwise with detachment and without complaint, since whatever melancholy or happiness he has was irrevocably ordained by the deeds of a previous life, and his complicity in that situation will doubtless help next time. It stands to reason, therefore, that a sweeper or a shoemaker – or for that matter a woman, all equally starcrossed – will have started off with a debit balance from the former life; a priest or a Cabinet Minister will have been born well in credit. It is the *dharma* of the sweeper to squat at the feet of the Minister to redress in this life the accountancy of the last one; if he does it dutifully and unprotestingly enough he may himself be a Minister the next time round. On the other hand, if the total of the Minister's good deeds falls short of the cosmic norm he may well be reborn as a sweeper himself, or even a woman. No one can escape from the cycle of *dharma*, and must pursue it without envy if he be poor, and without self-criticism if he be rich.

This age-old and barbaric philosophy maintained the debased Indian victims in the gutter and most of my well-heeled commercial and official Indian acquaintances in comfort, with the Government of India endlessly preaching the betterment of the one and leaving untouched the establishment of the other, and this is why India remains basically a country of the hungry and unhappy.

*

In our household we used to have spells of muttering balefully about the Brahmins, much as in my British circle at home we would mutter about the Tories – that is to say, less for what they were than for what they symbolised.

43

The social–political status of the Brahmin caste is very difficult to define. They can be (and in fact are) Prime Ministers, but they can also be (and indeed usually are) cooks, since anyone can eat what a Brahmin has touched, but Brahmins themselves are selective. My wife's family are not Brahmins; they are Kshatriyas, which is the warrior caste, and from time to time my wife remembers this.

Brahmins were originally the teachers, priests in a fashion. They alone knew the supernatural score. They could perform sacrifices in the correct way, knew the extraordinary combinations of formulae. They asked no more for their talents and services than that the public should feed them, house them, support them, and see that they wanted for nothing.

This the public did, because the Brahmins had tremendous spiritual pull. Anyone who behaved wrongly – i.e., anyone who was mean to a Brahmin – would be born again as a crocodile, or a mongoose, or an earthworm, and it would take him several generations to work himself back to human form. It was probably no sillier, and even more humane, than the Christian talk of hellfire and eternity.

The Brahmins themselves were safe enough, on the whole – they were already twice-born; they needed little saving, and they could not be promoted since they were on top of the stack anyhow. Equally nobody could be promoted to Brahmin in his lifetime, though it was just possible to make it in a couple of lifetimes hence if one behaved well and gave money to Brahmins. The old-style Brahmins were rather like the scientists of today.

The whole point of the Brahmins was that from the cradle to the fire they knew it all. They could choose brides and soulmates, they could propitiate the gods and intercede with the officials. Under the British they more or less ran the country; the bureaucracies were full of them. The British gave the orders; the Brahmin babus, despising the unwashed English, saw they were carried out. The Brahmins were the biggest con-men in the world. According to most of my family friends they still were. We got to seeing Brahmins under every bed, especially in Madras.

*

Aja knew everyone in town. My father-in-law had a great gift for friendship. He could not walk a hundred yards without being greeted by someone. He was a most improbable character to have been a police officer, which is what he had been in the days of the State; indeed he must have been in many ways the oddest policeman ever, since he had left not a whit of rancour behind him. A stroll with Aja took three times longer than with anyone else, so constantly was he hailed and drawn into conversation with some reputable citizen or, more likely, some former law-breaker whom he had sent to jail and whose family he had supported and protected thereafter. It was said of my father-in-law that Miscreants, as they were termed, vied with each other to get sent to the cooler at his instance, since he would then be seized with compassion and have the best of food delivered to the jail. Mama thought he was soft, and indeed he was, though not in the head.

Aja came from the very small southern state of Coorg, which had always been virtually unknown, or known at least only for its speciality, which was the production of senior soldiers and Police Officers. Why that should have been nobody could explain. Aja could recognise a fellow Coorgi from two hundred yards, albeit a total stranger. From time to time he would pause among the crowd and say: 'Ha. I knew that Coorg fellow's family,' and would summon him with the authority of former office, addressing him in the Kannada language. Long genealogical discussions would ensue. It happened to ricksha-drivers,

45

waiters, hotel clerks, policemen, anyone. He was never wrong.

At all events my father-in-law had the widest catalogue of acquaintances in town, and among them was Philip.

Philip's real name was Ana Aseervatham. He had two friends whom he valued more than any : one of them was my father-in-law and the other was the late Earl Attlee.

More than four decades earlier Ana Aseervatham had been a registered conductor-bearer, accredited to the then British Government of India. In this role he had chanced to be assigned to the Simon Commission when it came to India in 1927. This Commission had been set up by Lord Birkenhead, Secretary of State for India, with the ostensible purpose of investigating possible reforms in the Raj, but with Lord Birkenhead's firm intention to see that reform should be the last thing to arise. To this end, he appointed as Chairman the charmless and arid lawyer Sir John Simon, whose refrigerated personality was a guarantee against goodwill. The Labour Party, still far from office, compliantly appointed as their representatives only obscure back-benchers. Among them, however, was Mr Clement Attlee, which was not without relevance to the momentous events of twenty years later.

Ana Aseervatham, who had now become the more manageable Philip, found himself looking after Clement Attlee, as guide, valet, and factotum. It must have been an odd relationship, but it endured. For thirty years they kept it alive.

In 1950 Philip, back in Bangalore, fell on hard times. There was no place for registered conductor-bearers in the independent nation. Philip's idea now was to open a bar, since Mysore state had at least escaped the bane of prohibition. For this it was necessary to obtain a licence. Philip wrote to Mr Attlee. Mr Attlee wrote to Sir Ramaswamy Mudaliar, who had been Dewan of Mysore. Philip got his licence.

In 1956 Attlee was the guest of the Indian Government. Before he arrived he wrote to Mr Nehru. Mr Nehru wrote to the Home Minister in Mysore. Philip was rediscovered, sent to meet Attlee in Bombay. Together they toured India, with Philip once more in his old role.

They continued to write to each other until Lord Attlee's death. Philip produced for me a great file of letters, cards, gifts, from Downing Street, from the House of Lords, from Great Missenden.

It is a curious thing that a country so concerned with memorabilia, so obsessed with imagery and symbolism, so conscious of its independence, should in all its enormous space have found no crack nor corner to mark the name of the man who in a sense engineered that independence. The names of Viceroys good and bad were commemorated in a hundred streets, now indeed mostly renamed for father-figures more recent and appropriate – but for Clement Attlee, Prime Minister of the Raj who surrendered the Raj, there was never a street nor a statue nor a stamp nor, it sometimes seemed, even a memory.

Except perhaps for one: the Requiem Mass that is held once every year in an empty St Francis Xavier Church in Bangalore, which is paid for by Ana Aseervatham, known as Philip.

*

I was never quite sure what was the language Aja had been born to speak; he seemed to be at home in so many. The South Indian languages are dauntingly difficult. They are of the Dravidian group – Tamil, Telugu, Kannada – and nobody outside South India can make head nor tail of them. Other Indians tend to think of them as obscure

47

tribal tongues, despite the fact that they are spoken by more than sixty million people, and are probably the oldest language group in the subcontinent.

Languages interest me very much – as the rock basis of communication, and in their own aesthetic right – but I have never been very good at learning them. I was reared as a child in France and I grew up effortlessly bilingual (and how fast it fades) and my trade obliged me to be able to skate through the superficialities in one or two of the easier forms of speech. But I fear life will be too short to learn to come to terms with a Tamil.

There are fourteen separate and recognised languages in India and (the experts will only guess) about two hundred and eighty dialects. After Independence it was ordained that 'the national language of India shall be Hindi'. It was not, it never became so, and it never will.

Hindi is the language spoken around the Capital and is from Sanskrit. It is written in the Devangari script, which many of the others are not. The Moghuls arrived and ruled India from Delhi; they spoke Persian. Some sort of mutual language had to be evolved, and this was Urdhu – a mixture of Persian and Hindi that eventually evolved a classicism in its own right. When the British came they characteristically invented yet a third form of speech, which was called 'Hindustani'. As a language this had few parallels anywhere, since it was contrived to be spoken between rulers and ruled, and is useful only for the giving of commands.

As a young learner of journalism in the India of the 40s, I was zealous enough to feel inadequate without some means of talking to and understanding those about me. I bought an elaborate book called *Hindustani Self-Taught*, and spent long hours in its study. I worked up a hesitant acquaintance with the simpler clichés. If I wanted a bath at seven I could bring myself to say : '*Ham sat baje guram*

48

gusal maingte hain.' If I wanted a message delivered I said : '*Chithi lejao aur jawab lao.*' When repeated often enough and loudly enough, and if I waved an envelope in my hand and gestured urgently towards the street, the phrase worked wonders; the chaprassi would nod eagerly and say : 'Okay, sahib want letter taken.'

I felt as one always does in a new country the need to go a little farther than this and to be able to articulate the few courtesies that might indicate, at the least, goodwill. My phrase-book, however, suffered from the incurable complaint of all phrase-books designed for communication between masters and servant; it was unable to think otherwise than in brusque and peremptory commands. 'Keep quiet. Come here. Go away. Cook more quickly and more better the tiffin. Wash more. Wake up. Stand still. Bring me instantly tea/coffee/whisky-soda/ammunition/good shirts/vinegar. Do not lie to me. Go. Stay. Withdraw.'

There was no tense but the imperative, no mood but the irascible. The work had been 'Specially Composed for Visiting Persons and Allied Officers' by a Mr H. Achmed Ismail. There was a daunting section on 'The Engagement of Body-Servants' : 'Look sharp. Come tomorrow. Shut the door. What is your pay? It is too much. I shall pay you far less. Put on the fan. Put off the fan. If you break crockeries I shall cut your pay. You feign sickness. You are indeed dirty, make clean yourself. You are underdone. You are too old, too young. I shall engage another bearer.'

After this grimly one-sided conversation the matter, one felt, could only end by having the candidate shot from a cannon's mouth.

Even in the 'Sickness' section Mr Ismail maintained an impatient, choleric manner. 'The bowel is distracted. The tongue is hairy. I demand my teeth to be drawn.'

The personality of the embittered Mr Ismail permeated the book as with a wry satisfaction he put into the master's

49

hands every assistance to their natural bad manners.

'Hindustani' hopefully began to fade with the Raj, as perhaps one day Pijjin will fade from the Pacific. The official assumption that Hindi, albeit a real language, could be imposed on all the Gujeratis and Marathas and Oriyas and Malayalams and Telugus and Kannadas and the rest was a loser from the start. There were riots and sit-ins and gheraos until Delhi conceded that two hundred million people could not necessarily be wrong and accepted their linguistic autonomies – autonomies that may one day demand cession. But that, I think, will not be in my time.

4

TALKING TO my cousin Anand was like talking to a highly educated three-year-old child, or perhaps an intellectual grasshopper. It has always interested me that the Indian people, who can produce yogis and mystics capable of meditation for weeks on the precise nature and configuration of their own navels, can produce such huge numbers of people totally incapable of concentrating on anything whatever for twenty seconds at a time. Anand is such a one – charming, well intentioned, enthusiastic, volatile.

'Quick, tell me about it, I must know every detail.'

I have not said ten words before he is calling out: 'Usha, did that letter come? How much I need it. – But go on, I *must* know your feelings on the matter.' Another twenty words, then: 'Gita, we have too much of fan; also where is Sami, I think he is up to mischief. – Yes, yes, go on, go on, I am absorbed.' A moment later: 'Not to interrupt, did you see George in Calcutta? He was there on a meeting, most interesting, I must tell you. But go on, go on; I cannot wait.'

Eyes straying, thoughts darting. Suddenly I see his eye has fallen on something in the paper: 'No, this is really extraordinary ... but later; tell me what you were saying.' In the end no sort of communication is achieved at all, except an erratic and generalised goodwill. I go away leaving Anand with the warm feeling of a conversation rounded off and consummated, of which he is happily not obliged to remember one word.

I came to the conclusion some time ago that conversation, as others understand it, does not exist in India. Indians grouped in public places – waiting-rooms, buses, restaurants, air terminals – feel obliged to address one another in a kind of controlled scream, a high querulous monotone pitched at a level of open-air oratory, which of course has a self-increasing factor. The one speaker will continue to talk, in what seems to be a mood of unvaried protest and complaint, while his hearers fall into trance-like states until he is momentarily checked by some interruption a few decibels higher than his own. Someone else will instantly take up the theme, while the first speaker relapses into a reverie, or gazes absently about him, or picks up a newspaper. I cannot remember ever hearing between Indians what would pass elsewhere for a dialogue. The Indian genius is for rhetoric, not repartee, for assertion, not discussion. Perhaps this explains in some degree the morbid sterility of their politics. A professional politician in India does not change his mind, he changes his Party. He shifts one area of monologue for another.

Explicitly social occasions are a different matter. The Indian heart of hospitality is as a rule almost limitless, but Indian small talk is the smallest in the world. Party conversation at a formal middle-class reception has a strange period charm, so faithfully does it parody the dafter conventions of the English scene of, I suppose, the Frederick Lonsdale era. It encapsulates the mimicry, by now wholly established, in which Indian middle-class pretensions are rooted, the mimicry that does not flatter the society it imitates but unconsciously mocks it, since it is the imitation of an imitation, a mirror-image at two removes. All the Debs who have become Dannys, the Jaminis who became Jimmys, the inescapable ubiquitous Bunnys and Buntys with their eager fading slang, the Army officers who are Sandhurst caricatures down to the last detail of manner-ism and moustache, the last phrase of hearty jargon – only after a long time does it dawn upon one that the whole scene is a chimera. This is mimicry of a high order, but it is not of England, or even of the English; it is an impersonation of a fantasy. The curious rites being acted out are based not on a Raj that ever existed, but a Raj that was called into being in the imaginations of both sides, the fictional dreamland of an 'Anglo-India' with its Sahibs and its Mems and its Gunga Dins and Mrs Hauksbees : a parody of a parody. The weird thing is that it never did exist until it vanished, leaving this eerie simulacrum behind.

It is too easy to mock it – and mercilessly is it mocked, most bitterly by the educated patriots who resent the charade while sardonically joining in the act of rejection. For that is how they would define it : the expensive company apartment, the tailored suit, the gin and tonics are part of the vehicle in which the prosperous middle class, itself part of a bold inheritance of an independent India, can withdraw from that India. And, worse deny it; in their ruefully humorous Sahib-style despair of their country's confusions they necessarily align themselves with its detractors, and therefore add to those confusions.

Nor can this withdrawal be other than bogus; they may deride their roots but they can never lose them. They go far too deep into the antique soil to be totally disguised behind a dry martini and a Harrow tie. Bunny and Betty will welcome you readily into their handsome apartment that could be, as it strives to be, the best of Bayswater, though enough components of the décor will be Indian to reveal good taste. Wives and husbands, men and women, mix effortlessly among the guests. Yet the marriage of Bunny and Betty was arranged, when they were Rammonohar and Vijayalakshmi, and their children's marriages will be arranged, after careful consultation with the family astrologer and the company accountant. And the party will not be halfway through before you will be aware of the inevitable phenomenon: the human ingredients of this graceful mélange of the sexes have somehow come to bits, the men convivially massed at one end of the room, talking the gossip of money, the women protectively grouped along the far wall, chattering the gossip of the *Onlooker*. Already the traditional segregation is as complete as a public lavatory.

And the gossip is without malice or pleasure, without wit or cruelty, without anything, revealing no prejudices nor passion; it too is a ritual. The latest political scandal will be discussed with neither disapproval nor envy, not even with any artistic savour of the scandalous, merely as something to say, rather than say nothing.

The new visitor is a momentary prize. An Indian gathering will always welcome him with a far more genuinely unaffected warmth than would a European one. The interest will not be simulated nor the greetings faked.

'Hullo, what part of the world you coming from?' This is inevitable; the question comes point-blank, with a smile; it is the accepted introduction. It is no more irrelevant than the routines with which Anglo-Saxons get an encounter off the ground: is there a more futile phrase than 'How do you do?' The Indian gambit likewise does not require information, only recognition; your answer is equally a formality. 'Hullo, what part of the world you coming from?' 'Hullo, from Outer Mongolia.' 'Very nice place there, let's meet again, bye-bye.'

The new visitor who is now demonstrably half of an inter-racial marriage merits even greater interest, and usually kindness. 'Hullo, you are Moni's husband, how *very* nice. And how are you finding India?' The temptation to reply: Just as I have always done man and boy for twenty-five years. Instead you murmur: 'Lovely. But my

54

dear, so *hot* this time; I could *die*.' The Indians are far more obsessed with the weather than are the English – possibly with more reason. Is it a mark of gentle breeding to express hatred of the heat? I don't think so; paradoxically I think Indians are genuinely more oppressed by their summers than are strangers. Perhaps the cruelty of the Indian sun has vitiated their ancestral fibres for too long.

'Please have a curry-puff. Is not too spicy for you?'

How many years more will I have to come here before people stop asking me: Can you manage Indian food?

After a while the gay chatter modulates into the Who Was That theme, soon to be recognised as the leitmotive of all such gatherings.

'No, that was Gita's mother's sister; she married Benni whose brother was your cousin Joshi's friend; you remember he married that Bombay-big-business-daughter, very nice though I must say a Parsi. What I am meaning is your uncle's father's second cousin, you *must* know her, they had the big place in District Road; it was divided among Sammy and his brother. You remember their children went to St Mary's with your other cousin Tara, who married – no, he died before, she married that other nice man; poor souls, they had three daughters and one became a Christian on account of Georgie. My dear very-nice-sari-I-must-say, was it costing a fortune? Never mind don't tell me, I shall be jealous, my husband can buy me nothing now what with cost-of-living and Government, really life is going-to-the-dogs, isn't it....'

Everyone is strikingly handsome. Middle-class Indian wives are technically supposed to be plump, or even corpulent, otherwise it might be supposed that they are unhappy and misused by their husbands. My wife is built on finer lines. The accepted comment on this is: 'My dear you are looking *weak*.' Even now this makes my wife, who is lissom and graceful, faintly uneasy.

55

It is wrong to feel that one could be back in Bayswater, however much it would gratify one's hostess to be told so. The alien concept endures because it was created from a fairy-tale. That is why some Indians will forever miss the Raj, which made so indelible an imprint and yet withdrew so effortlessly, almost so absent-mindedly; that is why there was no Indian Algeria; that is why part of India remembers its image of Britain while Britain has already forgotten India.

I never ruled in India; in another aspect of fantasy India came to rule me.

For myself there were times when I became aware of my otherness to the environment, of my personal graceless-ness of movement, a well-intentioned clumsiness of gesture, possibly even of thought. Even after twenty-five years of acquaintanceship with the surface mores of the country I am still caught out in somehow clodhopping attitudes. I think I could avoid the grosser solecisms, but I could never walk like an Indian. No European could imitate the extra-ordinary flexibility and manœuvrability of the Indian hands. Indians talk with their hands as they dance with their hands. There is none of the Latin shoulder-shrugging, eyebrow-raising, broad-swinging gestures, but a continual rippling of the palms and the fingers, with each nuance moulded out of the air, as though sculpturing syntax out of space.

I was continually learning something. The sari – the most elegant of garments, with an inscrutable architec-ture: Moni told me of its variants, its subtleties, the im-perceptible differences of folding that indicated its wearer's region.

'What does it mean if the sari falls over the *right* shoulder?'

'It never in any circumstances does. The whole point is not to inconvenience the right arm.'

I pointed out a woman no more than ten feet away whose sari fell over her right shoulder.

'Well. Must be a left-handed woman.'

This situation was familiar to me. On my very first visit so long ago I had been taken by a dedicated and bird-minded Old Hand through a relentless course of domestic fauna.

'Look quickly – the ring-necked parakeet. The speck in the sky is a white-back vulture; they eat Parsis. This pea-cock, very holy indeed, it represents the Lord Krishna – not this particular one, of course, it belongs to the hotel.' He flung a stick at the sacred fowl which rushed away screeching venomously. 'Now here's an absorbing sight – those little birds there; they are called the Seven Sisters. They are never to be seen except in groups of exactly seven.'

'I can see only five.'

'Strange. It must be a curious mutation.'

In years to come I was to observe the Seven Sisters birds in every grouping and combination from two to twelve, snapping and disputing with each other like ill-tempered old women. To the experts they are always curious muta-tions. So much in India is.

From time to time I would feel a pressing need for some sort of contact with world events. I suppose my life has conditioned me to this addiction, which is not wholly self-indulgent. Now it was uncommonly difficult to find out what was going on anywhere, at least if one had to depend on the English-language press, which was deplorable. It had not the purposeful concrete stubbornness of the com-munist press, nor the meretricious stupidity of the pop press of the West; it was just semi-literate, ill-argued, imitative; when it was not boring it was exasperating. The newspapers occasionally professed to be combating pressures from Government, which was quixotic, since the Indian press was a processing-plant for Government hand-outs, and for convoluted obfuscation Indian Government handouts have to be read to be believed, or otherwise, as the case may be. I must beg the pardon of my many Indian friends in our trade, some of whom are thoughtful and intelligent men, journalists in their own right (as is evident from the work they do outside), but they are enmeshed in a dismal machine, which grows worse every year.

All-India Radio was not much of a help either. When it could drag itself away from the playback singers of the Indian cinema, and when it offered news in English, it had, like the papers, a leaden obsession with the minutiae of politics, the pettifogging detail of Parliament, a pre-occupation with the machinery of government as distinct from the realities of democracy. Like the newspapers, it showed not the slightest knowledge of nor interest in the affairs of other places.

It finally came down to the short-wave band of my transistor, and I became ingenious at finding my way round the frequencies. The BBC world service was a refreshment, when I could get it, which was erratically. At the time relations between official India and the BBC were very frosty indeed; they had quarrelled over a television series on India by the Frenchman Louis Malle – a dispute in which both sides had behaved like obstinate children – and tuning in to Aunty had an agreeable feeling of conspiracy, like listening to a clandestine radio. This was compounded by the curious fact that the only place where my little set seemed to work efficiently was the lavatory. There I would sit at odd hours in the night among the disembodied and disjointed squeaks from God knows where. I sometimes wondered whether it was worth all that fiddling work to learn the winner of the 3.30 on the other side of the world.

On the other hand, China was all over the dial. Day and night it chirruped on in its mysterious Mandarin or Cantonese. When Peking radio went over to English its stuff was of a rich, obsessive silliness, like a sort of barmy John Bircher in reverse, a parody of itself. I would listen compulsively to this weird old-fashioned dialectic, the twittering rediscovery of the archaic soapbox clichés, the steadfast timeless indignation against Running Dogs, Lackeys, Revisionists and Bloodstained Imperialists. I love China and know it enough to feel slightly betrayed at all this sterile balderdash, the absolute lack of any understanding of the methodology of propaganda. Was it really impossible to promote the Maoist theory other than by this child's-primer phrasemaking, which would make any socialist cringe? Did they really want Indian intellectuals to listen to Chinese radio as a comedy act?

It did not really matter. Next day there was an advertisement in the Hindu:

Best Wishes to Madurai Corporation
Dr s. KALIMUT:U RMP (*Ind*) VVC
visits your town

All sorts of debility of men
Piles and Gas Troubles &C.

Treatment: Very high class: Rs 90/-
High Class: Rs 42/-
First Class: Rs 33/-
Second Class: Rs 24/-
Ordinary: Rs 17/-

At least there was no nonsense about equality with Dr Kalimathu.

As time went on I felt my curiosity about remote affairs diminishing. Things were to catch up with me in a big way by and by. For the time being, however, the small things mattered more.

One day we went to see Moni's guru, the soothsayer who lived in the old town. She was hesitant at letting me do this, though whether for my sake or the guru's was not clear. After some conspiratorial chats with Aja at the end of the garden, and vowing to keep the whole thing from Mama (who disapproved of the guru), the consultation was set up.

The guru's place of business was at the end of a narrow street off the bazaar. It was not difficult to locate. A small crowd of clients was already waiting in the compound; they had settled down patiently in the manner of Indian customers or supplicants everywhere in anterooms or the verandahs of lawyers, doctors, politicians, Government officials, giving the impression that they had not only been there a very long time but were prepared to wait for a day, a week, a year, forever. Surprisingly there were several Muslims.

There were signs in Kannada, Tamil, Hindi, Telugu, English, Urdhu. It was said that the swami was fluent in eleven languages. One sign said: 'THEFT WILL NOT BE PRE-DICTED.' Another: 'SPECIAL CONSULTATIONS WITH SPECAFIC ATTENTION TO THREE QUESTIONS: Rs. 6. DITTO WITH ATTEN-TION TO HOROSCOPE: Rs 10.'

There was a string of dried mango-leaves over the door, flanked by two Sanskrit swastikas.

'I SEKE NO FEES WHATEVER FROM REALLY POOR AND DESTI-TUTE WHO COME AND REQUIRE MAY ADVICE.'

An attendant must have spotted us, for we were beckoned in ahead of the waiting crowd; I felt deeply embarrassed but nobody took the least offence, making way for us with courteous smiles.

We were led into the guru's little room – white plastered walls with pictures of the Hindu deities, sacred scenes, an Air India calendar, the conventional zodiacal symbols, a poster for Mico spark-plugs. The sage sat on a bolster behind a long desk about two feet high piled with files, card-index boxes, and documents apparently covered with planetary indications. He rose to give us namaste, and greeted Moni. The last time he had seen her had been seven months before, but he instantly and effortlessly recalled her and the detailed subject of their conversation, though he must have seen tens of thousands of clients in all that time she had been living in Europe.

'I have continued to intercede for you at the three-quarter moon regularly.' He spoke in beautifully modulated English.

He said to me, in the businesslike way of a family lawyer: 'There is a religious basis, obviously. But principally scientific. I do not believe in numerology; it is nonsense. Phrenology is a science, physiognomy is a science, palmistry is in some senses a science, though not all. I hardly ever use any of these things. What we shall do is as follows. Write down three questions. They can be of any nature you like.'

An assistant was at my side with a clipboard on which was a single sheet of paper.

I was unprepared for this. It occurred to me that this could possibly be an experiment in thought-transference, or some kind of extra-sensory communication. If this were so, then to write down questions that were of genuinely immediately importance to me, that had long been stacked in my mind, would make it too easy, since if the swami had this perceptive talent he might well be already aware of them. At the same time it would be insulting to write down frivolities, or to attempt a trick. I felt I had little time to reflect on this dilemma (thinking of the waiting crowd outside) but it seemed significant not to waste the occasion on triviality.

I decided to submit questions originally posed in classical form by others, yet which has in a way become associated with me. I took my pencil and wrote on the paper:

1. I have read that the most important part of a journey is the point of departure? True?

2. Ovid wrote: '*Video meliora proboque, deteriora sequor.*' (I had used this once in a book: I see the right path to follow, yet I take the wrong one.) Why should this be?

3. (This one was real.) Where shall I finally make my home?

I folded the paper into an envelope, sealed it, gave it to the servant, who took it to the desk. The guru touched the closed envelope very lightly with his fingertips, for perhaps three or four seconds. He consulted a chart of Sanskrit symbols from the modern filing-box on his desk. He thought for at most half a minute.

'The first answer is not wholly evasive. You ask if the value of a journey is determined by the point of departure.' (He had got the key phrase.) 'Clearly not; the importance is in the destination, the arrival. I think I can assure you that the journey you contemplate will be successful, at least partially.'

I had contemplated merely going to Ooty for the weekend, a few miles away.

At once he said: 'I do not mean your immediate brief journey; I mean the major journey which everyone undertakes with a new life.'

So far, very good.

'Secondly, you ask why, when confronted with two alternative roads, you recognise the better one, yet choose the worse.' This was a fantastic bull's eye. 'It isn't a new question, nor perhaps originally phrased.' He glanced over his glasses; his second sight was having me on. 'Nevertheless is a very real dilemma, very common for you. The fact that you asked the question means you recognise your aptitude for error. Also measure of perversity. You will make the mistake less, are already making it less.

'Third: you will not make your home where you were born. I cannot be more exact. You will have alternatives. I can say: you will not die at home.'

'Thank you, swami-ji.'

'Any time, dear sir.'

I went away baffled; Moni content. There had been absolutely not the slightest question of trickery, legerder-main, mirrors, double-writing, codes. There had not been time, for one thing; he had brushed a sealed envelope with his fingertips. He had answered the questions, in two cases out of three with perfect accuracy, in the third a ninety-nine per cent pass. He was most clearly a mind-reader, whatever that means. He made no claim for the supernatural – maybe supra-natural; anyhow extraordin-ary. The man had special antennae. It was emphasised by the wholly matter-of-fact way he did his business, his efficiency, his economy of action. Obviously his skull con-tained some quite improbable dimensions.

But what a mind to have! How – I demanded as we tramped back through the bazaar – did he contrive to conduct his *ordinary* life, if at every meeting he must see through normal encounters and social stratagems into the real mind underneath? Did he on entering his place of business switch himself on to some sort of psychic over-drive, engaged only in office hours? Then when he re-turned to the banalities of home, wife and family switch himself back to neutral? Why did he not go raving mad?

I was so burdened with these considerations that I ob-liged Moni to take me to see him once again, this time in his home. It was a grievous disenchantment. He lived in a mess of room-filling icons and knick-knacks, appalling oleographs, airport art; a shrine like a junk-shop. Contemplation there would be like meditation in a Chelsea boutique. He no longer talked in the crisp wonderful specifics of our consultations, but in empty fortune-teller's phrases.

'Communism will be destroyed by 20 October 1974.'

'As you know, the philosopher Albert Einstein recommended exploding atomic bombs to shift the world back from its angle of twenty-three degrees to the upright.'

'Why?'

'For special spiritual reasons.'

'I don't understand.'

'Nor ever will you.'

*

It was necessary to arrange a rendezvous in New Delhi with a colleague who, being a photographer, was naturally staying in the multi-star Ashoka, which we were not. We went to send a telegram. This is always a convoluted process, calling for a heavy drain on the emotions. To send a telegram in the ordinary public fashion necessitates at least four separate but interrelated operations. You approach the counter, which is besieged by a shrilling gesticulating crowd, waving papers and calling out imprecations. You seek for a form on which to write your message; there is none in sight. A tattered person bears down upon you, crying: 'Sahib, sahib, here formies!' thrusting into your hand a crumpled selection of applications for wireless licences, registration claims, and instructions as to what to do in case of fire. He will finally produce a telegram blank from the depths of his costume, holding firmly on to his half of it until some small reward has changed hands. You then stand with your message in a surging undisciplined crowd of fellow-customers to have the words counted. You then form up on the outskirts of another anxious multitude to pay your money. You then transfer to yet another group to collect your receipt. The entire procedure can take up to thirty or forty minutes, at the end of which you emerge wan and shaken, with a strong conviction that your telegram's future depends on a series of the blindest chances.

Halfway through this performance I collided with authority. 'Leaving Friday,' I had written, 'hoping foregather with you weekend.' The clerk, a sombre youth with steel-rimmed glasses, demurred at the word 'foregather'.

'Is not being proper English word.'

'Oh, but yes.'

'Is not being proper English word. No good.'

'I assure you it is a proper English word with a specific meaning. It means....'

'I am telling you.'

Weak as I was with heat and frustration, I felt this was a compelling challenge.

'I *know* about being proper English word. Please send telegram.'

The clerk put a small sweetmeat into his mouth, climbed slowly from his tall stool and sauntered into the back shadows. After a decent interval he returned, climbed with leisure back into his seat, adjusted the sacred string round his neck, and pushed my message to one side. He showed neither rancour nor triumph.

'Babu says not being proper English word. Next persons, please.'

The crowd behind surged happily forward; the debate was clearly over. I wondered in a desultory way how my message had been sub-edited, in what shape it would turn up in Delhi. I need not have worried; naturally it never turned up at all.

Yet another odd encounter awaited. Outside the office there appeared a middle-aged man in the crumpled khaki drill of all lowlier officers in some sort of Government employment. He approached me smiling, like an old friend. He said, astonishingly, that he had been the Passport Inspector who had checked our papers on our arrival at Bombay on such and such a day, whenever it had been. What a pleasure it was, he said, to meet me again, and in such an unexpected venue. Uncommonly gratified by being remembered out of hundreds of airline customers, I wished him the time of day very cordially indeed, and asked what brought him so far away from his post of duty at the immigration desk at Santa Cruz, Bombay.

This would seem to have provided his cue. It appeared his son was far from well and in some up-country hospital; he had to catch a bus that afternoon. Through some complicated mischance he found himself without his wallet: could I, for old times' sake, give him the loan of fifteen rupees for two days? He would of course require the name of our hotel and our room-number so that he might return the loan; without that he could not of course accept the money.

Every sign pointed to my being egregiously conned, and I have been conned so variously and in so many parts of the world that if anyone can recognise these portents I can, which at the same time has never protected me from their consequences. The frank and open candour of the man's guileless face did, to be sure, proclaim dishonesty. At the same time how could he possibly have known when we had arrived at an airport hundreds of miles away? Why was it of importance to know our address? Could he have been, by some chance, really a Passport Inspector? It seemed to me that fifteen rupees was not too high a price for finding out.

But unfortunately the telegraph office had cleaned me

out; I was therefore obliged to go to the car and ask Moni to lend *me* fifteen rupees – and, of course, to explain why. My responses to this kind of situation are not shared by her, and perhaps with reason. It was her opinion that I was being taken for a mug, in the crudest way, and with her fifteen chips. I said that the man's ingenious scripting was surely worth the money – moreover I believed he would repay it, indeed I would bet on it. If he failed me I would give her back her fifteen rupees two-fold. Perhaps not that: I would give her back twenty.

The man took the money with warm thanks but without the effusiveness of a con-man's gratitude and walked off with dignity. Naturally he never came near us to pay it back, and Moni collected her score. But this was not to say that I never saw him again.

Many weeks later and after many a long journey, I was crossing a road near the same hotel when I recognised him. Simultaneously he quite obviously recognised me. Yet contrary to all the rules he did not avert his eyes and duck round a corner; on the contrary he stopped and waved, with a broad smile of welcome from that transcendentally candid and mendacious face. I felt a warm admiration for this remarkable humbug. I wondered what he could find to say, now that the Passport Inspector gambit had exhausted its usefulness.

There was no doubting the sincerity of his pleasure at our meeting. Why, had he not been this very day on his way to call and repay his debt – ten rupees, I think? No, fifteen. Alas, it was of no consequence, since misfortune had again visited him and but an hour ago he had been obliged to disburse his last rupee on medicines. His son, I hoped, improved? The face, wiped now of its artless optimism, assumed the lines of inconsolable sorrow: *this* was his problem, god had ordained that this day he must return to the hospital; there was this question of the fare....

I shook him warmly by the hand, into which I pressed the only rupee I had with me, and wished him well in his career among the passports. A momentary bewilderment flickered over that protean face, but it was instantly replaced by a grin that, for once, I believed to be sincere.

'Salaam, nuzoor!'

'Salaam, Inspector Sahib.'

I have absolutely no doubt at all that when, or perhaps if, I ever return he will be there, watchful and irrepressibly resourceful, to reinforce my affectionate faith in the changeless East.

*

'How much more British you are than I,' I said to my wife. We were driving up through the Nilgiri foothills towards Ootacamund. It was the archetypal relic of the former British hill-station; it had been to the South what Simla had been to the North – more so, it was as Bognor to Bournemouth. Nobody ever called it anything but Ooty. 'As a girl,' I said, 'you went to Ooty for your holidays. When I was discovering India I never went to Ooty because that was where the English went. I wanted to see where the Indians went for their holidays.'

'Indians never have holidays. Those that do, those who could afford to go anywhere went to Ooty.'

I knew about Ootacamund from legend and hearsay, and especially from Molly Panter-Downes' *Ooty Preserved*, the only book I ever read celebrating the posh past and final old age of a Raj hill-resort. The book was done with such felicity and affection, and Moni had been talking about the place with such nostalgia, that now we were in the neighbourhood (as you reckon things in India) there was no escaping Ooty now.

We passed through Mysore City, which I found ex-

68

tremely forgettable except for the extraordinary vision of St Philomena's Church – a great Victorian affair in the Bombay Gothic taste contributed by the Maharaja in 1933, which seemed an uncommonly civil thing for a Hindu ruler to do in the middle of his own bailiwick. The names of the sponsors were on the walls, around the pillars, along the catacombs, everywhere, tens of thousands of them: Christians, Hindus, Muslims, Sikhs. It seemed a pity that this outburst of ecumenism had resulted in what must be unchallengeably the most hideous church ever built.

We wound upward through the forest. Deep among those trees were tiger, leopard, elephant; nothing stirred but once, when a great porcupine scurried clattering across the road almost under the wheels. It grew perceptibly cooler. Ooty lies at seven and a half thousand feet. Then the country opened out, and suddenly became exotic. That is to say, it began to look exactly like a sort of Sussex. One realised why the English had settled so unerringly on this place: more and more it resembled the South Downs. Or could a hundred and fifty years of the Raj somehow have transmuted the region into its own likeness?

Edward Lear, visiting Ootacamund in 1870, had mysteriously compared it with, of all places, Leatherhead. As we grew nearer the town I began to understand why.

Rather, however, did it resemble a place like Camberley, say, or an embryonic East Grinstead. There, eleven degrees north of the Equator, were the suburban villas with the Victoria gables, little spines of cheveaux-de-frise, the neat hedges, the rustic nameplates on the gates: *Glencoe, The Nook, Heatherleigh, Windermere*. The tidy gardens had flowers like stocks, and Canterbury Bells. One knew without looking that behind the mock-leaded windows would be chintz and cretonne, and doubtless ceramic ducks.

Then, abruptly, a statue of Gandhi and a small shrine. Some mad aberration, or some strange bitter irony, had placed it at the very entrance to a cordite factory.

We passed a group of uniformed schoolboys – brown faces above blue blazers, khaki shorts: a penitentiary colour scheme.

The centre of town was called Charing Cross.

Most of the hotels had closed down. We were staying, by courtesy of the Army, in the military inspection-house at Wellington, a mile or two outside. Colonel Bedi, a tall Sikh with the smile of a film-star, received us with the utmost charm and hospitality, for all that he had never clapped eyes on us before in his life, and took us to the Officers' Mess.

The Raj had not retreated an inch, not a minute; 1947 might never have been. Kipling lived again, sitting in those leather chairs, under those high ceilings, among those walls hung with sporting prints, hunting scenes, views of Somerset villages, among the glass cases full of silver cups, regimental memorabilia; the friendly young officers in the billiard-room chaffing – yes, *chaffing* – each other with I-say-jolly-good-show, and Really-Billy-you-are-a-one!

It was downright cruelty to smile, and yet one smiled, because *they* smiled – innocently, generously; they were too young to have known any of those old white colonels and burra-sahibs whose fading portraits drowsed sternly from the walls, and in whose day not one of them would have been so gracefully lounging there with the little pegs of whisky that would last them the evening. It was heart-breakingly true: Kipling had left it all behind, even in the epilogue of the national inheritance. The whole Imperial episode had been a play; it had overrun its time and now the understudies had taken over, darker in the face and more graceful in gesture, but indistinguishable in the lines they read and the moves they made – indistinguishable, too, in their interpretation of the role, their part in the architecture of an India which has never lived without rulers, each ruler intuitively assuming the pattern of the one before.

However, in the British days of that Mess we might not have been as kindly used.

That evening we sat on the little terrace of our room. I love dusk in India more than anything else in the world. A gentle thunder was grumbling around the hills; the monsoon was not far off. The scent of the cypress hedges was everywhere. Half a mile away a herdsman was sitting on a hillside singing quietly to his cows – a long and seemingly formal song, inexpressibly soothing. I knew I should never belong to India, but at these times I came very near to it.

Thus I was unnaturally tolerant when the bath-water went wrong. The bath-water in hill-stations is always going wrong, but this was an eccentric malfunction, in that when the water went off it was the cold supply that stopped. Steaming water abounded, but it was far too hot to use. It was therefore necessary to fill a bucket with boiling water and allow it to cool, so that it could then be used to dilute the new hot water. The difficulty was that one would then decide to use the water-closet, which naturally would not flush until one had filled the cistern from the bucket. One thus lost one's spare supply, and had to refill the boiling bucket, again allowing it to cool, while preventing anyone from using the WC. The whole process took a very long time. But, for once, time was what we had in plenty.

It was an engaging paradox that this place, which once must have so assiduously cultivated its Home Counties image, was also the home of a tribe of aboriginals, called the Toda. The Toda, like the British, were a vanishing aspect of the landscape, but they still survived. They lived in *munds*, kennel-like dwellings with low doors; like the Masai of Kenya they had become tourist-attractions. People filmed them, recorded them, and annotated their customs, which had originally been extremely rude but had become modified under the pressure of so much examination. They were polyandrous, yet somehow contrived to maintain a system of patriarchy. They revered two main gods, a brother and sister called On and Tiekirzi, with five or six hundred others in reserve. They were both amiable and handsome, in an aquiline way. There were all manner of theories about their origins: some anthropological authorities detected in the Toda certain Sumerian links with ancient Mesopotamia, or they were refugees from the court of Ceylon, or they were a Lost Tribe of Israel, or they were surviving stragglers from the Macedonian soldiers of Alexander the Great, or they were simply part of the Dravidian stream that had retreated before the Aryans god knows how long ago. It was of little consequence to the Toda; the thousand or so who were left were diminishing yearly through the effects of inbreeding and syphilis. It was questionable what their views were about the disappearance of the British rulers; probably few of them were aware that they had ever arrived. The Toda were long accustomed to being despised, then tolerated, then preserved. Their philosophy seemed unarguable: they were in the business of fading away, a human attribute most unusual in India.

One of the young officers was good enough to tell me that I was an honorary member of their golf-club. I had in truth not played golf for more than twenty years. In my youth I had played a good deal in Scotland, where golf was the recreation of people of modest means; when I came to England and discovered that a golf club was both a luxury and a bore I abandoned the pastime instantly and without a moment's regret. However, here I was, a lifetime later, with time on my hands and a funny little empty hill golf-course, and on impulse I persuaded Moni to let me have a go. I had planned to hit a few shots at random here and there in isolation for old times' sake — I should have foreseen that this would be impossibly simple; there was no way of escaping a caddy, even a fore-caddy; accessories I had never used in all my life before. The whole silly enterprise took on a false kind of solemnity, and I felt both foolish and pretentious.

As usually happens after years away from a club, my first shot was a beauty. I had no reputation to maintain, no face to save, I wanted only if possible to hit something gentle and middle-aged and straight; I therefore drove with excessive copybook caution, and by some atavistic miracle the shot went like a bird. My caddie was impressed. I knew it would not happen again.

As we plodded on from hole to hole I became aware of a curious thing: the caddie tended to fiddle about with the ball, and improve my lie. At first I thought this might be simply an Indian formula of courtesy to strangers. With great embarrassment I took to looking vigorously in every direction other than where the caddie was nudging my ball into a better position, so that I could come upon it, as it were, with a clear conscience. But this was evidently not part of the caddie's campaign: when he became aware that I was deliberately not noticing his stratagem he would wait until I was about to address the ball and then *further* improve the lie, even to the extent of shifting the ball a couple of feet, making quite sure that I was taking note while he perched the ball delicately on the most propitious little tuffet. It was not enough that he was generously watching my interests for the sake of favours to come; it

73

had to be made abundantly clear that he was so doing. His dishonesty became almost farcical, and my compounding of it even worse. When it became clear all round that both of us were perfectly aware of the process, it simply became a matter of the caddie rearranging the ball and teeing it up wherever we were.

At first I would look around with a strong sense of guilt. By doing so I became aware that every caddie was doing the same thing to every player. So we were back to stage one: Indian pragmatism adapting itself even to the schoolboy ethics of a silly game: the object of the player is to hit good shots, the *dharma* of the caddy is therefore to assist to that end.... Later I learned that it *is* a local rule, sanctioned by the Committee: every player is allowed a given number of 'preferred lies'. It gave a new dimension to the word lie. It is of minimal importance now, since I shall not play golf again.

*

The nearby town of Coonoor clung to the hillside as though it were in danger of slipping off. It too gave the rock-pool impression of having been abandoned by the receding tide. Moni took me around it with increasing disenchantment; it was not as she had remembered.

Strange men moved about the streets in pairs – swaggering, arrogant, unusually costumed, with sombre challenging expressions.

'*Very* difficult people. Muslims. They are Pathan moneylenders.'

They looked quite mediaeval. They were in truth genuine Pathans from the mountainous borderland of the far North, traditionally the usurers, jobbers, moneylenders, colporteurs of rural India. At some time or other almost all the poor were in their debt. Now they lived continually in their Shylock makeup; ostentatiously they wore their tribal Pathan dress and puggri, their eyes painted to look fierce, their moustaches menacing, they stalked around the bazaar swinging heavy sticks; it was clear that they were feared, and hated, and rejoiced in the fact.

This was a terrible and apparently ineradicable part of the Indian economy: the almost universal dependence of the peasant on the moneylender, whose savage rates of interest were a lifelong nightmare to the poor. The usurers were either Pathans or Marwaris, Jains from Rajasthan.

Everything now was always reminding me of something else. I now suddenly recalled a moment from ten years earlier.... We had been making a film in Bengal about hunger. How appalling it sounds in retrospect: the exploitation of natural calamity for the sake of sixty minutes' television; all one can say is our motives were not wholly ignoble. Since this sort of thing can be better done by symbolism than statistics we were to personalise the whole catastrophe of Indian privation in one village and one peasant family, and such a one was found. As far as it has any meaning, he was in fact on the edge of starvation; natural conditions had been compounded by his debt to the local moneylender, the *bania*. It was not more than two hundred rupees, less than twenty pounds, but the moneylender's interest was an anna a month on each rupee, something like seventy per cent a year, and on his subsistence economy there was no earthly hope of him *ever* reducing the debt, let alone discharging it. He was one of millions whose life and miseries were, had been, and forever would be dominated by the spectre of this moneylender.

When the production was done the film people rewarded him for his time. How much did he owe the moneylender? It was paid. And should we say another hundred for a fee? It cost the company about one-eighth of half a

75

day's production costs; to this starving Bengali peasant it was a situation totally unprecedented, unimaginable; the Holy Grail had fallen into his hands.

'And now,' they said with infinite and patronising good humour, 'what will you do with the money?'

He looked at them with incomprehension. 'What will I do with it? What would you have me do?' He smiled for the first time probably in his hopeless life. 'Why – set up as a moneylender, what else?'

What else?

*

I am a faithful lover of railway trains, but there are few left to love: that is to say of the real kind that puff and hiss and grunt, with organic engines based on fire and water. One such remained nearby to us in Ooty: this was the Coonoor-to-Runnymede Express.

It was not in any technical sense a miniature railway, but it gave the impression of being so – its design was that of a toy train, one found it at a toy station, with a tiny Edwardian booking-office. Buying two tickets, however, turned into a transaction; they were only Rs 2.50 each, but for some reason they had to be made out with three carbon copies; the thing might have been an airline.

There was a waiting-room, and an 'Upper Subordinates' Rest Room' – a very Indian-type rank, that of the Upper Lower. Both had on the wall faded typescripts of the 'INVENTORY. Bench long with sink lined. Glass looking-on stand. Goat Stand. Hanging with wall. Mirror-fix wall. Long char rotten seat.'

'What *can* it mean?'

'Long chair with a rattan seat, stupid.'

'Like the Goat Stand.'

By and by we chuntered nicely off to Mattupalayam,

the junction for the main line. The platform was piled with oxygen cylinders, bicycles, baskets of fruit, cans of cinema films, sacks. There was the usual subdued hysteria while people manhandled their baggage on or off the train. Even on a minute journey like this nobody travels without a mountain of luggage.

The six little coaches were painted bright blue. The locomotive made a great fuss with clouds of smoke and steam, but did not move. All along the train heads popped out, shouting encouragement and advice. After a while half a dozen green flags were waved by conductors along the train; it seemed that someone in every separate coach had to signal the start – or rather endorse it, because we were on our way anyhow, with a sudden tremendous jerk.

There was another stop while we engaged the Rack. This was the cogwheel underneath the train that locked on the counterpart rail and would permit us to get up the steep gradients without sliding backwards to Coonoor. We began the climb with great caution and slowness.

Gradually we were overtaken by bullocks, very old men, small boys, once even by an immense blue butterfly. We could reach out and pluck dog-roses from beside the track. Stupendous views opened out over the Nilgiris to the plains. The warm air brought through the windows a long running buffet of scents: blossoms and resin. Every now and then we would pause for no particular reason.

At these pauses the passengers would climb out and defecate by the track. There was no especial hurry. One, slightly slower than the rest, got left behind. He leisurely completed what he had to do, adjusted his lunggi, and overtook the train without difficulty.

We got off at Runnymede, in the tea-garden country. We had travelled five kilometres. It had taken precisely one hour.

5

A TIMELY strike in the domestic airline obliged us to travel from Bombay to Delhi by train, this time a real train. I would not have had it otherwise. I long ago grew weary of travel, but trains still bring it nearest to pleasure.

India must be the one country where the railway is genuinely part of its folklore, a romantic institution seemingly built into its history which is not altogether an impossibility, since it was the railway that unified India in a way the soldiers and administrators could never have done. Has anyone ever written a learned affectionate study of this enormous organisation which compresses its interminable distances into an almost manageable size, the complexity of co-ordinating these thousands of miles through repeating patterns of confusion? It should be done; the railway is the supreme example of India resolving all her natural disorder and fallibility into a wholly acceptable success. Perhaps, indeed, her only one.

Catching the train at the terminus is the first adventure. The cab deposits us into a scene of tempestuous anarchy. It would seem that all the threshing energy of Bombay has reached a kind of focal point here, and saved for this moment – the furious crowds pressing with desperate and totally self-seeking urgency simultaneously in twenty directions, the hordes of contending sweating porters, red-turbaned and shirted the colour of brickdust, bent stick-like legs and arms raising vast burdens of metal trunks

78

and canvas bedrolls, the cries of the tea-vendors and the dealers in two-month-old copies of *Time Magazine*, the absolute certainty from the sight of this labyrinthine ferment that the train will never be found, let alone caught, that indeed it cannot possibly exist, and that if unbelievably it does exist no reservation could conceivably have penetrated this chaos.

And yet, at the end of the wild scramble through the multitude on the heels of the porters, dreading to take our eyes from the one recognisable bobbing vermilion turban on which the future of our luggage depends — there is the train, the carriage, the compartment, our names legibly on the door : we are there. It feels like a triumphant journey's end, not a departure.

This is the Frontier Mail; the stirring old names remain. It is due to leave at half-past six that evening. It leaves precisely at half-past six. We have twenty-five hours of splendid solitude before Delhi.

A friend of Moni's had exercised pull; we had a two-berth coupé. Somewhere down the length of the train the third-class customers were crushed in, fifty or sixty to a coach like a travelling henhouse, crawling about in dispute and recrimination until somehow they would settle down in a congested coma for the journey that might last them days.

We were better placed. We had been able to buy a night and a day of the greatest Indian luxury, which is isolation, privacy. Our coupé appeared to be fairly new, different from the little moving huts I remembered from long ago; its comparative modernity still did not quite compensate for the old-fashioned wooden Edwardian spaciousness. It had a corridor, so there was no way of ignoring the child next door who wept and complained for hours. Its bunks had bedding, of worn but spotless cotton. The washing-basin in the shower room had a plug on a chain just too short for it to reach the hole. Two electric bulbs had gone, so as the dusk closed in we gave up hope of reading. It mattered not at all; neither of us felt like reading on our first ride together on the Frontier Mail. We were quite childishly excited.

Without ostentatious haste the Indian train devours the distance. In Japan the Bullet Express projects you from Tokyo to Kyoto at a hundred and something miles an hour with the exactitude of a precision instrument; the Frontier Mail chunters along with the resolution of a mechanised bullock-cart, with the same random unexplained pauses and the same convulsive heaving starts; in a way both trains express the nature of their environment. The night came down, obliterating India.

We awoke as the sun was crawling up, drenching the land in the special dawn light that always suggests to me the colour of cinnamon. How much of Indian time' is spent awake at daybreak! The land drifted by in its repetitive hugeness: the inhabited desert. When you fly over the dry dun-coloured undulating wilderness of India it is hard to believe that this empty lunar landscape is part of an overpopulated world, this desolate waste; not a stream nor a caravan-trail to show that humanity exists in such desperate abundance. From fifteen thousand feet one looks idly out an hour later; one might never have moved.

On the surface, at the land's own level, everything is different. You are aware that you are never anywhere without sharing it with someone, or a hint of someone – the solitary figure already in the field, the women already at the well, the tenuous linking of human habitations. Villages appear and recede, indistinguishably. Rural India has no tradition of domestic architecture; it has no endurance so it has no age. The homes are built of mud and vegetation, by and by they will dissolve back into mud and mulch, they will recycle themselves inconspicuously back into their natural components as will their inhabitants; this is as it should be.

The railway stations give the lie to all this timelessness. Every now and again we stop at platforms seething with all the shrill concentrated life of miles around. Every wayside station has the appearance of an incipient civil war, with its ceaseless battle for the pumps – still always two, Hindu and Muslim, with a vestigial tap somewhere at the end for the untouchables; this is discouraged by law and less and less observed, but the symbols remain. The train is besieged by wailing processions of beggars, fruit merchants, vendors of *pan*, dealers of rice and curries and tea. The food is eaten from plates of banana-leaf, the cups are of baked clay, both will be thrown later from the carriage window without a twinge of conscience, very quickly they too will rot and dissolve back into the soil from which they came.

So the sun climbs high and stares from a baking grey sky, heat without real light, we travel under a fine canopy of dust from the Sind desert that traps the windless sweat; when we drag down the window the solid air drives in like the breath from an oven. We smile wanly at each other and phew! – this, too, is as it should be; we are sharing India again. The heat oppresses Moni more than it does me, but I am showing bravado.

At one station there was more than usual commotion and an immensely hairy swami was ushered into the train surrounded by a court of diligent disciples. He appeared to be a man of comfortable middle age, obese and glossy and robust; nevertheless they upheld and supported his portly frame as if sustaining some fragile work of art; they settled him gently in his seat with many a genuflection and *namaste*. One acolyte reverently brushed the tangled mass of hair from the holy fellow's brow, another fell to massaging the short muscular legs.

It seemed there had been a meeting in the neighbourhood of the All-India Union of Saints and Holy Persons. (Let it not be said that the Indian nation was incapable of organisation; in Barnagar in Madhya Pradesh they had recently concluded the All-India Conference of United Hermaphrodites and Others.)

Our train now had the honour of conveying one of the Holy Person delegates home. The long carriage at once filled with a press of admirers, shoving each other viciously aside to touch the swami's feet, now visibly shod in new black oxford shoes and short blue socks. He accepted these ministrations passively, belching gently from time to time. Faces pressed against the window outside, an occasional fingertip groped through the opening to finger the homespun of his robe.

During all this performance the swami evinced no response of any kind, ignoring all the murmured hosannahs, accepting whatever happened to him without acknowledgement or protest, with an unchanging seraphic, slightly dotty smile. Once he expectorated accurately between his feet.

Finally, the whistle blew and the devotees reluctantly bowed themselves out. One of the passengers, a neat man with a briefcase still slightly under the influence of the *dharshan*, said to us : 'You are luck-ee. To have visit from swamiji. He is being famous saint from Karnatake, extremely hol-ee. He is regional delegate. *Most* good man.'

On arrival at New Delhi there was the customary chaos. The porters with our luggage put the cases on a trolley, whereupon a Railway Policeman advanced on them snarling and beat them off savagely with his cane; it appeared that the trolley was for the use of the swami. Our luggage was shoved on to the ground, and the swami's enamelled tin trunk was placed on it and wheeled away behind the holy man, now garlanded anew, and now revealed as even more adipose and graceless than he had seemed. He allowed himself to be supported tenderly down the platform, still wearing his mindless saintly smile. I got the impression he was somewhat drunk.

The station was Bombay all over again – a screeching competitive incoherence out of which order could never come, but did. We found a taxi.

'Maharani Barg, *malum*?'

Of course the driver didn't *malum*, he didn't know; nevertheless he set off at a roaring optimistic pace: God would guide him to Maharani Barg. The apartment we had been loaned – again thanks to Moni we had the use of a friend's company flat, a heart-lifting economy – was somewhere or other in one of New Delhi's development 'colonies', residential estates vaguely occupational in character (Diplomatic Colony, Defence Colony, Friends Colony, and so on) that had accreted round the periphery of Lutyens' original design in exuberant experiments in modernity, the kind of housing estates that will look always half-finished and tentative however long they exist. They have the incoherence of an Indian village translated into square-edged masonry; the dust of India blows around them but here it is the grey of concrete, cement, unmade roads, treeless and transitory. Somehow we found our house and spilled our exhaustion about the new home: the end of every journey, every day, is a small triumph.

*

New Delhi. I am always charmed by the consideration that this vast shop-window of a place is marginally younger than I. I was just six months old when George V and Queen Mary laid its foundation-stone on the Durbar site north of the old city of Shahjehanabad and announced that the seat of Imperial Government was now to be transferred from Calcutta to the ancient capital of Moghul India. This was by no means to everyone's taste; the big white business houses of Bengal, taken by surprise, were greatly outraged and chagrined at the threat to their investments. Lord Curzon denounced the waste of money; old tales were revived about Delhi being the 'graveyard of dynasties' – which indeed it was, as is demonstrated by the seven previously ruined Delhis lying all around.

However, the complaints of the boxwallahs had no effect on the big day in December 1911, when the Queen wore a crown allegedly fitted with six thousand diamonds, twenty-two emeralds, four rubies and four sapphires, when twenty-two thousand troops were paraded before fifty thousand people, with a salute of a hundred guns and a lavish distribution of decorations all around. There was, of course, as yet no Capital. The site was to be examined by a Captain Swinton – one of the London County Council, of all things – who was to give an LCC imprimatur to what would be New Delhi.

As it turned out it was to be nothing of the kind. The Westminster-wallah pronounced the site useless. Another was picked, south of Delhi, centred on the low escarpment called Raisina Hill, where land was both barren and cheap. In the darkness of night the foundation-stone so sumptuously laid by the monarch was quietly dug up, loaded onto a bullock-cart and moved ten miles away.

The Royal Institute of British Architects, required to recommend a designer for this momentous project, chose Edwin Landseer Lutyens, forty-two years old and up and coming. In his turn he selected Herbert Baker as his colleague. Lord Hardinge was set in his view that all the coming artifacts of State – Secretariat, Council Halls, Vice-regal Lodge, everything – should be built 'Indian style', whatever he may have meant by that. Consequently Lutyens and Baker were swiftly taken round India on a crash-course of subcontinental architecture and pointed at the recognised treasures – the temples of the South, the Palaces of Rajputana, the Buddhist stupas of Sarnath and, of course, the Taj Mahal.

The inspiration failed to take. 'Personally,' wrote Lutyens, 'I do not believe there *is* any Indian architecture. These are just spurts of various mushroom dynasties.' Baker accepted that there was a certain whimsical charm in Indian building, but argued that all this exuberant stuff 'did not have the constructive and geometric qualities necessary to embody the idea of law and order which has been produced out of chaos by British administration.' They decided on the inevitable Establishment compromise, making concessions to the Viceregal taste by grafting on to the drawings odd features of Indian style – the *jali* lattice-window, the *chajja* sunbreak, the *chattri* dome – which in the end were embodied in the looming Imperial complexes, with the exasperating and somewhat patronising result we now beheld and with which the Indian Government will forever more be lumbered.

The great gestation of New Delhi was fraught with trouble. Lutyens and Baker squabbled bitterly over details. The collection of the stone was a terrible business; it had to be quarried from all over the place – red stone from Bharatpur, white from Dholpur, marble from Alwar, Baroda, Ajmer. Ten years later it was still turning up. The site became the biggest stone-yard in the world. In the sheds were three and a half thousand masons. Kilns sprang up everywhere to turn out seven hundred million bricks. Five hundred varieties of trees were cultivated in the nurseries at Safdarjung. Thirty thousand workers mixed cement, hewed rocks, carried loads. The contractors arrived, staked their claims, grew quickly rich – first the Sindhis, then the Punjabis, laying down the foundations not only of the great new Capital of Empire but of personal fortunes which have endured and multiplied.

The whole affair was formally opened by Lord Irwin in 1931. That was just forty years before.

The New Delhi, itself created as an enormous Imperial emblem, was now a jumble-sale of little emblems of small authority : the labels. Official New Delhi was a gallery of blackboards, the labyrinth of a civil service that had to be reminded at every turn where it was in black and white – literally so; however self-evident the purpose of an establishment, it must carry its label, white letters on black : Ministry of This, Department of That, Sub-District Office, District Supervisor, stark boards of sudden ugliness placed so effectively to deface whatever amenity or merit the building possessed that for a long time I had believed they were temporary indications for some interim period, like contractors' signs. Years had passed, the labels remained, and new ones appeared; the blackboard had set its own tradition and become its own ancestor. There will always be old buildings needing new labels, more civil servants awaiting more hardboard cubicles, more contractors contracting, more grey blocks arising haphazard to make Lutyens squirm in his grave arising behind tangles of surrealist scaffolding. How is it possible that out of this wild bird's-nest of leaning bamboo-poles, without one straight line nor a vertical nor a right-angle, swarming with naked acrobats, can emerge a conventional fore-and-aft thing that would' look undistinguished in Uxbridge ? It always happens, and the result is always less interesting and adventurous than the wild wooden webbing that produced it. What about the grand design of the broad scrupulous boulevards, the calculated vistas, the monumental enormity of open space, everything at least a mile from everything else? It was still there. No jerrybuilder's enthusiasm to fulfil the Ministries' demands for their Sub-Departmental Annexes could overwhelm Imperial Delhi even in twenty-five years, but they were doing their best.

A local paper carried an advertisement for a night-spot:

> Step in LIDO
> for rich Pabulum
> Cabaret by Cockitish Cuckla
> & Radiant Axona
> Latest Wave in Capital.

I have a perverse affection for New Delhi, for it was there in my youth I met India head-on at its great crescendo. But Moni loves New Delhi more than I; she remembers it with a young woman's pleasure in a middle-class society where all the high gears meshed, where it all worked. She more than most was part of the political machinery throbbing all around, but it was of less immediate concern to her in her Indian twenties than to me in my European forties. I – knowing so little, learning so painfully slowly – had in a way been part of the machinery too.

Once Moni had lived here in a high-grade official bungalow across the way from Claridge's hotel, a modest place where I have sometimes stayed. I never asked how Claridge's came by its resounding name; presumably by some sort of reflected mimicry of the clichés of opulence that would have prevented it calling itself Brown's or, unthinkably, Rajendra's or Lal's. The world, after all, is littered with Savoys, Crillons, Ritzes, Bristols. Claridges in New Delhi was always good to me; the only criticism I ever had was the address. In Moni's day it was not there – or perhaps it had been something else; why should she remember? In those days you did not have to know these things.

I, on the other hand, had spent my life in hotels; I was an itinerant tenant of the temporary with my own peculiar but not demanding values. There was a time – pre-chainstore-caravanserai, pre-Hilton, before the days of the battery-hen traveller who is packaged round the world in successively identical environments – when I was very nearly a one-man directory of hotels good and awful and unspeakable. Over the years I became arguably one of the authorities on bad hotels, almost all of them to be found in former British colonial possessions, where the indifference of English railway-station catering – or occasionally NAAFI-culture – had come to terms with various forms of local sloth or hatred in a malign synthesis of the glum and second-rate. That, of course, was once upon a time, when one was perforce a traveller; travellers have now the haloes of tourists and pay for themselves and have to be treated at least as tenderly as they would be in Milwaukee, and if possible indistinguishably.

When I had first come to New Delhi, a few weeks before the British Cabinet Mission that was to solve all problems, conciliate all contention, and find overnight the blueprint for the glorious withdrawal of the Raj, I was to begin with unable to get a room in the Imperial, which was a serious blow to my self-esteem. The Imperial in New Delhi was then (and how things had changed today, when Moni and I came back!) the local Grand Babylon; it was perhaps the most excruciatingly overcrowded hotel in the hemisphere. It was – and indeed still is – vast and square, resembling then, as a heatstruck American remarked, one of the wartime factories the Russians moved to the Urals. It was full to the doors with a fluctuating tide of politicians, princes, newspapermen, idealists, cynics, black marketeers, beards, turbans, uniforms, sweat, Australian whisky, and obsessed fanatics of all persuasions. The apocalypse was expected momentarily; any day now Liberty would drop from the skies into a thousand concentric circles of speculation and propaganda.

The place smelled then, as now, of a penetrating mélange of patchouli and floor-polish. I was beguiled to find, on my sentimental return with Moni, that, diminished as it was, the old Imperial had not surrendered its wonderful Mansion Polish reek.

My wife and I walked through its lobby again, and for once it was I and not Moni who could soak in its Indian nostalgia.

There were so many new pleasures in those early days. Everything was of course pain-pleasure; there is no happiness in India without regret, but of this I was barely aware when for the first time I came to Delhi and found, as better men have found, no room at the inn, or at least not in the Imperial. Instead I bestowed myself in Old Delhi, in the Cecil – and the Cecil cushioned me sweetly from everything of truth. My room opened onto a courtyard almost filled with a pool in which the waterlilies grew and from which at night the fine fat frogs sent out their uxorious honking which so maddens some people but which to me is a most satisfying sound, the deep *onkh-onkh* which is that of the Tibetan horns on the Himalayan passes, and of the fat frogs in a Delhi pond.

But before night fell I would walk into town by the Kashmiri Gate, or down towards the Jumna River; it mattered little to me, everything was new and everything was wonderful. There was a time they called the cow-dust hour. The term came from the villages, as everything in India does, but here, walking along the Ridge, anywhere around the perimeter of the Delhi walls, it just meant the vague blue haze through a hundred trees, the smoke of a thousand evening mealtime fires, a thousand Indian wives crouching over chapattis and dhal on mudbrick stoves, the scent of the burning fuel-dung, the spectral cawing of the crows, homeward bound like us all. It was preposterously romanticised and possibly even dishonest, but it was my first knowledge of India and it never left my mind.

It survived even the Cecil and its proprietress Miss Hotz.

Miss Hotz was a lady of Swiss roots and British Raj conditioning; she ran what the Navy would have called a very tight ship, even for those strange class-bound days of the forties. We lived in the heartland of India, yet Indians (at least below the rank of Maharaja) were politely turned away; Miss Hotz tended to a belief that all Eastern people cleaned their fingernails with the cutlery. It was an odd indoctrination for me.

Many years later, in the course of making a film about India, I thought nostalgia warranted a return to the Cecil. It was, as I should have known, no more. It had been turned into a Roman Catholic Boys' School, called Saint Xavier's or some such; it was now institutionalised beyond belief, or even the dreams of Miss Hotz; everything was there but nothing was there. The little boys marched about in military order under the barking discipline of a seminarian; when I asked to see my old apartment, where I had learned the nature of my Indian bewilderment under a churning fan, I was shown an air-conditioned classroom crammed with desks; the sedge had withered from the pond and no frogs honked.

Perhaps one is obliged to believe that what has gone before was better – however unacceptable it had been it had been comprehensible. Now that I shall never return to the Cecil I foolishly rue it, and yet it represented everything I deplored then and regret today.

From Old Delhi to New Delhi was five miles in distance and about a century and a half in time. Twice, often three times a day I had to do the sweltering journey past the redstone Fort and the monuments to the concrete geometry of capital administration, past the bullock-carts towards the Packards, out of imperialism into the Imperial. Now with Moni I was doing it again, peopling this rather gaunt corridor with the fantasies of long ago – the enthusiasms and despair, the furious argument, the generosity and suspicion, the wrangling from room to room, the over-statement of emotion that insisted on the most common-place questions being resolved by gropings into obscure philosophy.

It was all diminished now. Places far greater and grander than the Imperial had arisen and overtaken it. The years had also in a strange way swallowed New Delhi – or perhaps New Delhi had swallowed them in its planless random growth. But in those days everyone who meant anything in Indian affairs was there, milling around in this great Oriental Ealing. One made long rounds of calls, perfecting routine pleasantries and standardised observa-tions. There was Jawaharlal Nehru, intense and unrelaxed, short-tempered, broodingly handsome, perhaps the most cultivated and beguiling politician in the world. Maulana Azad, the bearded scholarly Congress Muslim; he would talk only through an interpreter, pulling the man up sharply when he suspected a mistranslation. Vallabhbhai Patel, the 'iron-man' of the Right. The emaciated and exquisitely tailored Mohammed Ali Jinnah, the inflexible Muslim Leaguer and apostle of Pakistan, he who had, it was said, a difficulty for every solution. They revolved like planets in their own orbits, each with his circling retinue of satellites, experts, advisers, camp-followers, front-men. It was my first crash-course in Indian affairs.

I became aware – almost for the first really acute time of my life – of the phenomenon of racial antagonism, the normal peace-time aversion of one many for another for no other reason than that there was a difference of birth, of ethnic background. If that seems a singular naïveté then I suspect I had always been ingenuous in that respect; hav-ing been obliged to live so much among people of different races and allegiances I had somehow come to accept the premise that if any racial oddity existed in my immediate environment it would be me, and that would seldom work to my advantage. Things have not greatly changed, nor have I.

Finally, as the prima donna's entrance is contrived to just the right degree of expectant impatience, Gandhi had appeared, with a gentle simplicity and rigid austerity that had taken hundreds of important people many a hard rupee to organise. The Mahatma with his entourage arrived, by the only special train in the world composed wholly of third-class carriages, at Nizamuddin Station, far outside the main city, and once again that deprecating, ancient yet nimble little figure conjured up the multitude as he always had done, no matter where he might be nor what he might do.

As one of his mystic–political gestures he had decided to live among the Untouchables, to exert his unchallengeable authority from a headquarters in a sweeper's hut. By this he would demonstrate again his championship of the fifty-one million, as they were then, whom Hinduism had excluded from all spiritual hope, the Untouchables whom the British called the Scheduled Castes and whom Gandhi called the Harijans – the Elect of God, who spent, and despite much listless legislation still spend, a brief and tedious life on their haunches brushing the streets, or as washermen and barbers and shoemakers. An analysis of their extraordinary social position, I was told, in my innocence, would involve every aspect of abstruse tradition and economic injustice. The Municipality had built for them a colony of hutments in the Reading Road, by the Temple of Balmiki. There Gandhi was to join them.

It would clearly have been too simple a proposition altogether for no more to be done than have a sweeper move out and Gandhi move in. I visited him on the first day with his old friend and collaborator the late Mrs Sarojini Naidu, the poetess, politician, socialite, ex-prisoner and wit, the merriest Hindu rebel who ever came out of Girton.

We walked along the new redstone road that had been laid between the *bhangi* hutments, among the silent crowd of off-duty sweepers, responding to any gentle word with the soundless withdrawal that rose from many generations of remoteness.

The rest-hut of the Temple was converted to the Mahatma's living-room, with electric light, fans, telephones, bathrooms. It was there that Mrs Naidu made the immortal remark that over the years has come to be claimed as the personal experience of countless chroniclers, but which I steadfastly claim to be originally mine alone.

'Ah,' said Mrs Naidu, surveying this elegant scene, the only Untouchable Quarter in India with all modern conveniences, 'if the Mahatma only knew what it costs *us* for him to live the simple life.'

Moni is cynical of the story. 'It is a chestnut. I grew up with it.'

Useless to plead that even chestnuts have some original source, that she is fortunate to be married to this story's only true begetter; she remains unconvinced, as I fear do many others. I make a resolution, not for the first time, to write and express nothing that cannot be verified from the files. Within an hour I break my resolution; I continue to do so. I become a rich source of ancient Sanskrit sayings, spurious quotations from unheard-of holy verses, glimpses of encapsulated archaic wisdom improvised on the spot. Very soon nobody believes a word I say, even when by chance it lapses into truth.

What a year that had been; what a baptism into Imperial politics, with the fading Raj at grips with its inescapable moment of truth, and the deadline closing in. There was a wonderful sense of climax, a stimulating atmosphere of

93

urgency. Then suddenly the whole troupe, the entire dramatis personae of the Talks had decided that it was no longer humanly possible to burrow through the political maze in the intolerable oven of New Delhi, where the heat made it hard to rationalise even such problems as whether or not to cross the road, whether to stand up or sit down. So, quite abruptly, the whole company of this intricate road-show – Ministers, advisers, Congressmen, Leaguers, Viceroy, Gandhi, and a hundred or so newspapermen, all complete with entourages – found itself transported to Simla, the Victorian resort clinging to the Himalayan foothills, found itself toiling up killing gradients, found itself living in desperately intimate proximity, gasping slightly in the rare atmosphere of seven thousand feet, found itself at long last on the very edge of winding up Imperial India. Life became packed with the acutest interest.

Nothing anyone had done in India had been so difficult. For seven weeks the Cabinet Mission had been talking, pleading, reasoning, even threatening, trying to reconcile the irreconcilable. This was the payoff. There were no more secrets. Everyone had known for months the inflexibility of the two great camps, both demanding independence, but on no terms other than their own – Congress for a united India, the Muslim League for Pakistan, the Ulsterised India; both attitudes had been argued endlessly, incessantly, with a monstrous, monotonous insistence. Jawaharlal Nehru told me: 'After many years of experience and strife, I am almost achieving the condition of detachment.'

Simla was everything one had imagined it would be. It seemed satisfying that this final conference should be held in the one town which, with New Delhi itself, symbolised the things that were past. At this time of year it had been filled with old ladies and leathery colonels so true to type as to be almost unbelievable, sahibs and mem-sahibs who even then seemed scarcely aware that their world was on the point of dissolution. They moved with a vague, loitering air in this extravagant new scene impregnated with politics, among Congress chiefs like Roman senators in sweeping togas, among strident processions of Congress Volunteers and Muslim League Youth. And among and through this shifting variety moved the silent, ragged, shaven-skulled transport coolies, roped to impossible burdens, labouring along roads that never seemed to lead anywhere but uphill.

It was a troublesome town to work in; everyone of importance appeared to live at the remotest end of long lanes or the topmost summits of hills; there was no way of getting about (since the automobile was then banned in Simla) except on foot or in a ricksha which, because of the thin air and the frailty of the coolies, had to be pulled and pushed by four gasping, coughing men; an inexpressibly degrading experience. I circumvented this necessity by hiring a horse, and clattered with much pleasure from one HQ to another. It was in this fashion that I first came to know Jawaharlal Nehru.

Mr Nehru also had this idea of riding to work. He was an excellent horseman, and was to be found at all odd times of day trotting briskly around on a gay little piebald pony. No one else, it seemed, had a mind to ride, so we took to bearing each other company; thus I formed an acquaintance with a man whom as the years went on I was increasingly to admire, and even revere, until the final tragic days. From Pandit Nehru I learned more about India than from anyone, and a great deal about writing, and even more about the essential sadness of power. He was profoundly responsible for the achievement of Indian independence, and alas even more responsible in time to come for its vitiation and decay. Jawaharlal Nehru made

India, and lost it. He could have done with India anything he wished, but he let it wither, and at last it destroyed him. But he was always very kind to me.

None of these forebodings haunted the crystal air of Simla.

The one magical moment of the day was dawn. I would crawl out into the pearly haze at five in the morning, collect the horse and ride slowly out to see Gandhi, sometimes with Nehru, but he was usually earlier than I. Gandhi lived further away than anyone, in a rather commonplace furnished bungalow called Chadwick, at the end of a five-mile track. There, as the sun touched the spine of the hills, the High Command of the All India Congress would meet, and plan the day's strategy, and consider, and meditate.

It was a strange scene. On the verandah would be Nehru, shrugging into his brown achkan against the early chill, the impassive swathed figure of the enigmatic Vallabhbhai Patel, the mountainous, biblical bulk of Khan Abdul Ghaffar Khan, with his face like an Assyrian warrior, and curled up almost invisibly among them the little brown Mahatma. They would stand there, and walk in silence up and down, communicating, it seemed, through a sort of empathy, while the sun climbed higher and the vapours rose from the dank lawns. It was an Old Testament spectacle. At a certain moment the spell would break; they would fold hands to each other and leave; for a while Gandhi would sit alone, until his noiseless white-robed acolytes would glide around and bear him away to his baths, his food, his massage, his interminable writings.

On such an occasion I went to see him in his room: pale varnished wood, bare linoleum, the bleak decoration of any furnished room anywhere. I had prepared a few of the solemn-sounding, meaningless questions journalists are supposed to present to famous people, a purely formal gesture, a ritual excuse for personal contact. He answered patiently, a little restlessly.

'It must surely be appreciated by now that my belief in *satyagraha*, in non-violence, is an active thing, a militant thing in its way. It is possible for a violent man to become a non-violent man, but never for a coward. The political question is nearing its end; let us see a little further. All life implies some sort of violence; we must select the path involving the least. But there again you must go a little deeper....'

All the time the stooping, self-effacing girls in white saris moved soundlessly in and out; they brought nothing and they carried nothing away; their movements seemed only to fulfil some need within them to circle aimlessly in the presence, to justify their discipleship.

After a while Gandhi would slip his feet into his chapals, extricate himself from the conversation with some gentle donnish joke: an old man's joke. His eyes wrinkled with some secret pleasure, and then suddenly lost all contact with the moment, peering round the room for a secretary. Everybody would come in and once I found myself drinking orange-juice out of a cracked teacup.

I paid one extraordinary visit to Mr Jinnah, whose steely personality seemed to dominate the situation more every day. Mohammed Ali Jinnah, the Muslim Leaguer, was a negotiator of an inflexibility almost unique in a land of devious and serpentine minds. Every Indian suggestion met with his adamantine veto, every day his statements grew briefer and curter until they seemed to contain nothing but the single word: Pakistan. There was something infuriatingly admirable about it. I talked with him in his study – an aquiline haggard figure of almost startling thinness; of all the contestants in this desperate confrontation he alone avoided Asian dress, wearing lounge suits of almost theatrical elegance and cut. So excessively beautiful and splendid were they, so razor-like the creases, so immaculate the linen, that they seemed somehow to diminish the personality within. Mr Jinnah's costume was far more memorable than his rhetoric, which was weary with repetition.

Halfway through our encounter a strange thing happened. Mr Jinnah, again propounding the imperative of the Islamic State, chanced to glance at his tailored wrists and went quite suddenly silent and pale. He excused himself abruptly and left the room. I assumed he had been taken unwell. In a moment he returned, completely equable, and picked up his notes.

'I am sorry for the interruption,' he said. 'My bearer –' he clenched his thin hands, 'my bearer, like a fool, had put the wrong cuff-links in my shirt. But never mind; it is well now.'

This conference-reporting was a sterile and difficult affair anyhow, an enervating form of journalism for which I felt I had none of the right gifts. It entailed endless manœuvring in the dark, picking up hints, invading the privacy of important individuals who received one coldly if one called and protested resentfully if one did not. The distraught group of men who were trying, by now in a sort of anguish, to find a future for the luckless millions of India shut themselves up in the most inaccessible room in all Asia, and India, frustrated by weeks of inconclusive comings and goings, was beginning visibly to chafe at the total screen of secrecy. The uninhibited India press, constrained in no way by irksome considerations of verifiable fact, announced every day more and more extravagant speculations.

Up there in Viceregal Lodge, a knobby piece of Victoriana clinging to a slope above an entrancing Himalayan view, the definite centre of things was, by necessity, the Viceroy, Lord Wavell.

I had as wrong an impression of Wavell as had most people, that is I took him to be a well-intentioned soldier sufficiently distinguished and unsuccessful to be shunted into Viceregal Lodge as an expendable final tenant, with the usual Anglo-Saxon tendency to favour Islam. It was said that he read poetry, which was unusual, and for pleasure, which was still more unexpected. He was a shy and introspective man, and diffidence in soldiers suggests arrogance; it was fairly clear that he had few people to talk to. It was only years later when I read his diary (*The Viceroy's Journal*, 1973) that I realised how aware he was all along of the impossibility of his situation, how really and poignantly he understood the miserable trick Churchill had played on him.

He had indeed been an unlucky commander in the field. Churchill had sacked him from the Western Desert; he had been given little help in Burma. By 1943 he was militarily discredited, and his appointment as Viceroy was an expression of Churchill's simultaneous contempt for Wavell and for the Indians. What we did not know in those days was how clearly Wavell was aware of this. Most of us, of course, still believed to some degree in the Churchill mythology, the illusion of the wartime paragon; it was a long time before the catalogue of prejudices and rancour and conceit and small ill-tempered bitternesses emerged from the idolatry. Archibald Wavell had the disadvantage from the very start of knowing the disparagement with which Churchill regarded the Viceregal job. 'He hates India and everything to do with it,' wrote Wavell, 'and as Leo Amery [the Secretary of State] said in a note he pushed across to me, "he knows as much of the Indian problem as George III did of the American colonies".'

Churchill was 'menacing and unpleasant', he 'worked himself into a tirade against Congress and all its works' and said that only over his dead body would any approach to Gandhi be made. Before Wavell even left for India it was manifest to him that the British Cabinet was dishonest in its expressed desire to make progress in India. 'You are being wafted to India', said Amery, 'on a wave of hot air.'

Wavell's journal of those early years grows increasingly bitter and despairing. It could not have been encouraging to be briefed by Linlithgow, the outgoing Viceroy, to the effect that between the stupidity of the Indians and the dishonesty of the British the Raj would be obliged to totter on for another thirty years. Within the year he had 'found HMG's attitude to India negligent, hostile and contemptuous to a degree I had not anticipated'. His correspondence with Churchill verged on the unreal, so uncontrollable was the Prime Minister's resentment at any hint of progress. In reply to a memorandum on contingency planning for the end of the war, 'Winston sent me a peevish telegram to ask why Gandhi hadn't died yet!' The wayward and irrational obstinacy of this fading old piece of folklore must have been evident in India years before it was forced on the attention even of Downing Street.

And if Churchill comes meanly out of all this hindsight Clement Attlee emerges little better. For years to come we were to sustain this conviction, or perhaps illusion, that Indian Independence was the crowning glory of the post-war Labour Government in Britain, monument to the obstinately courageous statesmanship of Mr Attlee. It was Attlee who sent this Cripps Mission to India somehow to persuade Congress and the Muslim League to come to terms in a united Central Government to which Britain could painlessly hand over. When Cripps failed, we understood, Attlee decided upon the dramatic risk, and announced an appointed day on which the Raj would end, thus forcing Jinnah and Nehru to accept their responsibilities. Only this act of calculated political courage, we believed, got

Britain out of the dilemma of ruling for years a country disintegrating into civil war.

According to Wavell's journals this is a total fallacy. Extraordinary as it would have seemed at the time, if any one man should have credit for insisting that the only way out of a deadlock was a deadline, that man was Wavell. And, so far from acknowledging this, Attlee summarily fired him for so insisting – only to find Mountbatten, his chosen successor, insisting on exactly the same thing, and refusing to take the Viceroy's job without it.

Attlee and his government caved in, it would seem, and thereafter continued to take the moral credit for what had been forced upon them, and Attlee riding into history on the back of Lord Mountbatten.

It is a commentary on the intuitive and investigatory skills of the journalists that of all these matters we knew nothing. We lived in a world of increasing tension around us and diminishing interest elsewhere, a bad situation for a reporter. It is unexpectedly easy to get bored with crisis. It was hard to see how with the best will in the world the debate could continue in that electric atmosphere, and the best will in the world was only too clearly not there. Perhaps the intimate contacts of Simla had done something to soften the personal antagonisms that gave political India its peculiarly emotional aspect. It seemed unlikely. I could not exactly define why it seemed important to me. As one so new to India I could hardly be said to be involved – so many years were to pass before that could be said – and as a newspaper man I should, I suppose, have been professionally stimulated by the likelihood of true conflict to come. On the contrary I felt immeasurably depressed.

One evening the three delegations met in Viceregal Lodge to admit their hopelessness. Two hours later it was all over; a British functionary came tearing down the hill sitting very upright in a swaying four-man ricksha clutching a briefcase, tumbling out at the hotel with the story of the mission's failure.

All that night the rival groups of Congress Volunteers and Muslim Youth marched around town in strident columns, flag-waving, slogan-chanting; all night long 'Jai Hind!' and 'Pakistan Zindabad!' grated round the hills, while battalions of infuriated Simla monkeys, aroused from sleep in the treetops, screamed imprecations and showered sticks on both sides impartially.

It seemed that overnight this unlucky town was a place to be abandoned as quickly as possible. I suddenly felt as sick of India as I have ever felt of anywhere. There would doubtless be weeks' more fussing in Delhi, more explanations, analyses, protests, prophecies, but I wanted to go home. I was discouraged and tired and inadequate; the next time I came to India, I knew, would be too late to recapture all I had missed; the next time would be for the inevitable blood and tears. I knew I would not be long in coming back. I never guessed how often.

I went to say goodbye to Jawaharlal Nehru.

'I hope things will go in peace.'

'So do I. I know no more than you.'

They did not go well, as we know. The terrible surgery that was done to the Indian continent cost a million lives and left a crude and horrible scar. Even then we could foresee it.

I think Jawaharlal Nehru was the most important man I ever met. Scores of intelligent and well-intentioned Indians have derided me for this, citing for me the vast fallibilities of the man and the national catastrophe of his decline. All this is true. As a national leader Nehru was cursed by his imagination. He was paralysed by his intellectual evaluation of alternatives. He was, to coin a platitude, such a genuine giant among pigmies; it fed his pride and made possible his eternal equivocations. His achievement as the first prime minister of this enormous shapeless nation was so great that we who so respected him maintained the momentum of our affection far too long, after his vacillations and arbitrary impatiences turned him – certainly against his own will – into an almost purposeless tyrant, torn by arrogance and love. In the end he was surrounded by courtiers, chosen by caprice for their past loyalty or personal influence, never for the quality of their basic policies, almost always because ridding himself of them would have reflected on his own judgment. Thus in his final days was Jawaharlal Nehru surrounded by incompetents and sycophants and corrupt men; he denounced religious sectarianism and yet closed his eyes to its flagrant exploitation in his party's interests; he knew only too well the dangers of corruption in his circle and remained silent while it flourished around him. He was a hopeless administrator, and refused to be relieved of the irritating and time-consuming detail of administration. So obsessed was he with the vision of the future that he could not bring himself to envisage or accept the dismaying futilities and dishonesties all around him. He was cursed with two strangely incompatible attributes: compassion and vanity. Thus, in the end, he could reign but never could bring himself to rule. And he was to me the most admirable, and potentially the most valuable, public man I have ever known, and I mourned at his death.

For once, on this new return to Delhi, I did not walk the appointed paths and seek a meeting with the Prime Minister. It would have been absurd and impertinent: I was involved in no political task, I had no question to ask Mrs Gandhi of the routine kind or to which she could have reasonably replied, and now my acquaintance with her was too fragile to admit of a social call, even if prime ministers had time for such things. I flinch from meetings with celebrities that cannot be disposed of in a few minutes, having as great an objection to wasting other people's time as for others wasting mine. Mrs Gandhi's family, her father and her sisters, had shown me much kindness and consideration in the days of their eminence. When I would call on Jawaharlal Nehru long ago Indira Gandhi was never far away, watchfully guarding her father's brief moments of privacy and rest. I have on my workroom wall a lovely signed photograph of Panditji, Indira and her son Rajiv walking in the Prime Minister's garden – the little boy scratching his ear, his mother smiling, Panditji staring thoughtfully at the ground. It was taken on that weekend – twenty years ago? – when I had paused in Delhi on the melancholy homeward journey from Korea, with a mind so tormented with conflicts and bitterness that I had broken the rule of never approaching busy men without a reason, feeling that Jawaharlal Nehru might perhaps understand the complexity of my dilemma.

He saw me, and at once perceived that I was in no state nor mood to talk of Five Year Plans nor Congress divisions: I had just left a war in which I felt that a cause, starting with only a marginal justice, had already begun to corrupt itself, and us, and me, and the world, and for trying to say this I had been accused with bitterness by many people I believed to be honest. I recall saying at the time that Pandit Nehru alone was the man who could take the curse off moral platitudes simply by believing in them. This would have been a poor reason for exchanging even more moral platitudes now with his daughter. I knew her older aunt, Mrs Vijayalakshmi Pandit, the most decorative High Commissioner London had known, and Nehru's younger sister Krishna Hutheesing had so often shared her Bombay home with me, as I my London one with her – poor Krishna known as Betty, now untimely dead; I miss her wicked humour and her casual generosities.

With important people in politics a known journalist

is at a peculiar disadvantage: whatever his credentials of harmlessness or goodwill he can never be accepted without a marginal doubt. If he is not writing today he may yet write tomorrow. It is a suspicion I understand, and perhaps with better reason than many who hold it, and I will squirm to avoid it. This is perhaps why I have so few political friends in high places, and so many in low.

These irrelevancies continued to intrude.... Now Jawaharlal Nehru is gone, and his successor Lal Bahadur Shastri is gone, and Nehru's daughter Indira presides over a fragmented Congress and a baffled India where ambition is more than accomplishment and profit more than probity; and yet, for all that, one day the values will return and a nation will arise – but God knows how, and God knows when.

And who, in any case, are we to criticise?

*

Every writer in Delhi knows Nirad Chaudhuri, the most celebrated unknown in the world.

I had an acquaintance – I would not dare call it more – with this extraordinarily perverse and touchy little genius for some time before I sought his help recently with a film I was making. This help I received in great measure, with all the engagingly arrogant humility, the wildly immodest self-deprecation for which in middle age he had become famous.

Nirad Chaudhuri was for me by far and away the most interesting and complicated English writer in contemporary India, if only because he carried upon his minute and birdlike shoulders the most enormous chip ever worn even by a misunderstood man of letters.

For years he had been writing in Bengali, which is not, despite Tagore, the most fruitful path to a world audience.

Then he produced his first book in English: *The Auto-biography of an Unknown Indian*. Its effect was fascinating. The book touched some sensitive nerve in the class of India which he most energetically despised – perhaps because, being part of it, he knew it too well – the Anglicised Middle Class. Until then, being what they were, they had been totally indifferent to him.

These people, as Nirad Chaudhuri was well aware, had not the slightest idea who they were or where they lived, seeking to be more English than Indian and yet proclaiming a political patriotism that specifically denied the basis of their upbringing. The *Unknown Indian* hit these people hard in the crotch with a calculated insolence. He dedicated the book 'To the British Empire . . .'.

The Indian intelligentsia instantly swallowed the bait and twittered with indignation. Having read no more than the dedication they did not appreciate that it was a monstrous tease and that, so far from being pro-Raj, it was quite simply about the most superb study of East Bengal ever written, and moreover written in an English very few Englishmen could even approach.

The *Autobiography of an Unknown Indian*, needless to say, did not do very well. The Government of India put it about that he was not to be published journalistically. Nirad Chaudhuri did not prosper. His poverty grew, and his pride with it. This was necessary for a man who cultivated a deliberately peculiar, not to say comic, public image. He is a tiny little gentleman just over five feet high, and he lives in the bazaar by the wall of Old Delhi in a little flat stuffed – it is the only word – with books in several languages on a tremendous variety of subjects. There he cultivates the oddest of double lives.

At home Nirad Chaudhuri is the expected figure of a Bengali writer, albeit smaller and frailer than one anticipated, wearing a *dhoti* and working on the floor. This is his very private persona. Whenever Mr Chaudhuri leaves the house he changes character, personality, attitude, costume. He wears a European suit with a collar and tie and boots and a most extraordinary Sahib's hat. This is Nirad Chaudhuri in defiance and challenge to the new self-conscious political India with its elaborate slogans and its khadi and Gandhi caps. It is his calculated and successful intention to be misunderstood. The more he is misunderstood and derided for his preposterous English reach-me-down rig the more it delights him; it is his revenge on the Indian intelligentsia. He is parodying, through his funny second-hand costuming, their less funny second-hand intellectual attitudes. This is the vengeance of the Unknown Indian, and it is in its way magnificent.

Nirad Chaudhuri is probably the most widely read and best informed individual I ever met. For a man who until middle age never left his own largely illiterate country his erudition is totally formidable. He delights in displaying it flagrantly; he is a tremendous show-off. He has, indeed, plenty to show off. There would seem not to be a work of importance in any European language with which he is not wholly familiar and from which he will not quote, at length, and whether you like it or not. He will tell you the better vintages of the most unobtainable wines. He will tell you where all the major theatres in London are to be found, and what they are playing. He will tell you about the Vedas, about Beowulf, about the Icelandic sagas, about the works of Stockhausen and the music of Kerala. Every spot of this bizarre encyclopedic mosaic of knowledge has been derived from his endless reading and a kind of miraculous memory. When he writes it is with a completely masterful grasp on the technicalities and rhythms of English, and if from time to time it glories exuberantly in recondite references and embellishes its style to the baroque at least it is more than most of us can do. His conceit is both abounding and endearing. Anyone else behaving with his cocky assurance would be intolerable, but coming from this wispy little fellow who fought so hard against so much, who never conceded an inch to his second-rate detractors, who transcended poverty and ridicule, who never achieved one thing he had not won, it is pretty sublime.

It was part of Nirad Chaudhuri's contrariness – or perhaps his honesty – that he reserves much of his greater admiration for, of all people, Rudyard Kipling. He lectured me long and formally on the virtues and qualities of the Kipling *œuvre* – which indeed are beginning now to make themselves felt in more expected quarters. Similarly he told me of his grave distaste for E. M. Forster. It was worse than distaste; it was displeasure. If one is reproved by Chaudhuri, one stays reproved.

It was not altogether easy to be sure whether these two judgments were part of the famous Chaudhuri act, the perversity of the author who, by a satirical dedication, maddened the intellectual patriots who never read the book that followed it, and who henceforth decided that if the middle-class smarties wanted to mock him as a *kala sahib* then he would mock them by dressing up like one, and showing off like one, keeping his true life and thoughts to himself, as befits the diarist of the Unknown Indian.

I am still unsure, but he somewhat changed my mind. I went back that night to *A Passage to India* again, in the old Penguin with the brittle pages and the broken back, and once again wondered at its bland skill, the sureness of its technical touch. But now I can readily understand Nirad Chaudhuri's dislike and even contempt for it, for its washy liberalism and its uneasily didactic editorialising in the author's interpolations (when Fielding's conscience is not explicit enough, Forster's takes over). It was not enough – I saw now, which twenty years ago I had missed – for the various conflicts of Imperialism to emerge through the story of the Caves, it was necessary to moralise, to talk of the 'Oriental mind'.

I seem to be the only person of my generation who never sat at the feet of, or even met, the late E. M. Forster, but everyone argues that the decent-chap Fielding was a vehicle for the decent-chap Forster, that his bitter parable of colonial arrogance and insensitivity was a heartcry for justice. It now seemed to me that Forster was fighting his own sahib-ness through every page. When he tells Fielding to say: 'Away from us, Indians go to seed at once' and 'Justice never satisfies them; that is why the British Empire rests on sand' he knows he is right; it just seemed significant that he had given those lines to his honest reforming Englishman and not to one of his Imperialist Aunt Sallies like Heaslop. I began to feel, as I had never done in my first admiration of *A Passage to India*, that it must have been for Forster quite a torment to write, so clearly did he recognise the crude unkindness of the Raj, and so easily could he perceive the Indian evasions and dishonesties that provoked them into their stock responses.

I came to agree with Nirad Chaudhuri: Forster must have disliked the Indians as much as did his fictional *koi hais*, but equally he disliked the sahibs as bitterly as did the Indians. His rationalisation of the dilemma is what made his book so absorbing to me even now, loafing under the fan in New Delhi – and after all it was written in 1924; it is a measure of its enterprise (if that is the word) that one has to remember how adventurous it must have been.

I think Nirad Chaudhuri's error is to judge Forster as though he had been writing in the 1940s, say; he was not writing for the India League or for Krishna Menon; he was making a novel of India, not *about* India, in the days of Stanley Baldwin and the Wembley Exhibition and the

death of Lenin and the arrival of Mussolini and the acceptance of the British Empire as a permanent factor in the
human order.

What Forster had against colonialism (since he .was a
novelist and not a pamphleteer) was its corruption of individual relations, its destruction of personality. What
irked Forster about the Raj was that it turned a silly
Indian like Aziz into a martyr and a silly Englishman like
Heaslop into a tyrant, and neither of them were fitted for
roles so important. His solution was that of all fairly im-
aginative and irresponsible people confronted with all
colonial anomalies: 'One touch of regret – not the canny
substitute but the true regret from the heart, would have
made Heaslop a different man and the British Raj a different institution.' Of course he was right, and especially
to flinch from the 'canny substitute', the easy duty to
which so many of us contributed so much spacious word-
age in our day.

At the same time by that passage alone it was clear that
Forster accepted the necessity of the white man's burden,
that if somebody had to carry the can for the boring business of governing the British bureaucrat was the best man
for it – if he could be persuaded to do it with pats on the
back rather than kicks up the arse. And this was the fallacy,
since such a thing has never been possible.

Since the days of the *Unknown Indian* Nirad Chaudhuri
has found success. His *Passage to England* was probably
the first book by an Indian to sell out in Britain. He is no
longer ignored in Delhi; on the contrary he has become
something of a celebrity, even a social lion. 'Nirad stories'
became the currency of the dinner-tables. Mr Chaudhuri,
however, continues to live by the Delhi wall among his
groaning bookshelves.

I greatly wish I could read as much, and remember as
much, as that little Nirad Chaudhuri. I know I shall never

be able to do that. I remember something of C. E. Montague's in which he wrote that for him (even for *him*!) going through a well-read world as meagrely furnished with solid reading as he himself felt was like entering a first-class hotel with no luggage but a rucksack: the personnel treat you with courteous contempt for your obvious lack of credentials. I must say I never found the world quite so punitive as that, but I know what he means. A familiarity with the great books is not to be had in my way. One is acquainted with them, as one is with a country through which one had driven or over which one has flown; one recognises the famous bits, the Sights, the Characters, the Three-star Situations, but little more than that, and even these memorable portions one has not chosen onself, but have had them offered by others, or even by the ODQ.

Even in my life, which has not been spent among the giants of literature, or even of Eng. Lit., the talk has turned to Dante or Hardy or Peacock or Landor or Marcuse or Vonnegut; when that happens I can either confess I have not read a line of any of them, penitently or defiantly as the situation requires, or trust to the ragbag of associations or quotations they evoke to pretend otherwise.

There was someone or other in *Marmion* who thanked Providence that no son of his could read or write except one, and he could not help it because he was a bishop. That is going a little far for my taste; I sometimes quite desperately wish that in my adult years I had read more, and more diligently. I wish I had not been a writer, so that I could have had time to read, and not fuss about with books that as Lamb said are not books but things in books' clothing – histories, references, encyclopedias, files, papers, all the things that in the end induce a blindness to print itself. And the journalist's neurotic feeling that one cannot write and read at the same time, and that if one is not writing one is losing precious time – a foolish fallacy, of course, since three-quarters of the time one squanders in writing second-rate (and often second-hand) stuff would have been far better invested in reading something of value.

Bacon wrote: 'If a man read little, he had needs have much cunning, to seem to know that he doth not.' This is an excellent example – to drag effortlessly from the air an illustration from the concentration of a classic. And I do not even know where Bacon wrote it.

6

WHILE I was in India I had a job to do. Indeed it was this job, a magazine assignment, that had organised my passage, that would pay for my basic expenses while I was at work, that had in fact made the whole episode possible. It was almost like old times as a foreign correspondent, when one travelled in the best state one could contrive at someone else's cost. I have never been able to afford to journey much on my own account, since I had all my life been both improvident and baffled by money. I had never been conscious of any special extravagance; I supposed I wasted some substance on minor self-indulgence, but it was of the kind that left nothing behind; I had reached this age owning almost no possessions at all. I could never wholly understand how this had come to pass. It was clear enough that I had from time to time earned quite a lot of money, and managed it so ill that I still had no resources, nor was ever likely to have. It did not oppress me perhaps as much as it should have done; it merely clouded life with a basic anxiety that I took for granted. The fact that almost everyone of my acquaintance had organised their resources with far greater intelligence was a cause for admiration, not envy. That Moni had sought to cast in her lot with a financial organiser as clumsy as I remains a consideration of wonderment to me. Time was very soon to show how great her gamble had been, how soon her dependence on me was to turn into my dependence on her.

To justify my stay in India, then, I had to fulfil this job, which suited me very well indeed, since not only did it involve the mingling of serious politics with a certain amount of romantic flapdoodle, but the journey would take us through the heart of India where I had not been for years. The basic plan was to let me loose among the Maharajas at the precise moment of their disappearance, since Mrs Gandhi's government had finally cornered them.

The scenario went as follows: once upon a time there had been a Pride of Princes. (Even at the height of the Raj, India was only three-fifths British; more than half a million square miles were fairly autonomous States.) It had taken Independent India nearly twenty-five years to cotton on to the tenacious existence of these Princely anomalies in an allegedly democratic Republic, but they had come to the chop at last.

A great deal of dotty folklore had accreted around these curious monarchs and their life-style. According to certain legends these people in their day wore priceless gems for breakfast and conducted their daily business of despotism from the backs of elephants, in more-than-Oriental splendour. Another school of thought, mainly their own, held that the Indian princes were far-sighted and benevolent rulers and their disappearance mournful. However that may have been (and it was both), one might have thought to have heard the last of the Maharajas, but not so. Even in the tormented times that so threatened India today the princes stubbornly continued fighting on two fronts; against mythology on the one hand, and democracy on the other.

By the time we arrived the Maharajas had had a quarter of a century in which to adjust to the fact that their day was done. Only now, however, had they got the hard word: the Government was to abolish the Privy Purses and privileges they had enjoyed since 1947. They were

114

not going down without a struggle, irrelevant though they might be in the context of today.

Probably more nonsense was talked about the Princely Houses of India than about any comparable society – if indeed any comparable society ever existed. Their image was everything from the romantic to the ridiculous. Sometimes their wealth and power were fantastically exaggerated; sometimes they were in fact too fantastic to exaggerate. The eccentricities and outrages of some of these rulers became a kind of running fairytale; the diligence of others went generally unremarked. Much of the blame lay with the British, who made tools of them, then pets of them, and finally scapegoats of them. The poor old Princes, good and bad alike, were now up against a machine of which many of them had not the dimmest understanding; it was called Politics, or, alternatively, Mrs Indira Gandhi. India was left with a couple of hundred or so ex-monarchs defending a phantom heritage.

Their honorifics were variously exotic: Maharaja, Maharana, Nawab, Nizam, Jam Saheb and the rest. The late connoisseur of curiosities John Gunther was entranced to find that to address the Maharaja of Patiala correctly it was obligatory to insert in his mile-long name the word 'Sri' 108 times; in its brief form his title was Lieutenant-Colonel His Highness Farzand-i-Khas-i-Daudat-i-Inglishia Sri 108 Maharajadhiraj Mohinder Bahadur. Things had greatly changed.

At Independence, these people ruled about 100 million Indians. Many had their own armies, law courts, police; some their own Customs, postage, currency. Some were enormous; the Nizam of Hyderabad ruled a region as big as France. Some were petty squireens of a couple of square miles. In the days of the Raj the main railway line from Delhi to Bombay, almost a thousand miles, ran through only 150 miles of British India.

They had little in common. Some were very old – Udaipur was reigning in the Aravelli Mountains at the time of the Muslim conquest, Cochin had· been there for a thousand years. Some had bought their way into the club in Victorian times. Some looked after their dynastic interests with insight and integrity, others with a truly mediaeval selfishness. Here and there cropped up cases of wild misrule and turpitude. Yet Mysore and Travancore ran states more efficient and enlightened than much of British India.

Independence presented the Princes with a sort of Hobson's choice. Some rulers had been smart enough to see the writing on the wall long before, others were so dim they could not read it even yet. About half accepted compensation for their merger with the Union of India, the rest opted for Privy Purses and the retention of divers useful Privileges. It was these that they were about to lose, occasioning them great indignation, and us our reason for now setting forth from Delhi on the long road south.

These Princes' civil lists varied as greatly in their twilight as they had done in their ascendancy. There were half a dozen former rulers still drawing Privy Purses of more than a million rupees, or £55,000; eighteen pulling down between that and half a million, and so down the scale. The Maharaja of Mysore (an extremely austere and scholarly man) got a Purse of about £144,000 a year, tax free; the Maharajas of Baroda, Jaipur, Travancore, and Patiala got up to £90,000 and so on in a declining but scrupulously calculated scale until it reached rock-bottom in a strange, remote and elusive beneficiary, the Raja of Kotadia, whose Privy Purse of 192 rupees worked out at a fraction over ten pounds a year. This luckless man, who now bicycled to work as a municipal clerk in Gujerat, was ceremonially invited to occasions befitting his meagre standing, but complained that no one· ever sent him the fare.

The Nizam of Hyderabad, successor to that remarkable miser who was reputedly among the four richest men on earth, got less than half his predecessor's Purse, but was nevertheless worth more than £100,000 a year in public tax-free money alone. (The average Indian income is now reckoned at £48.)

The famous Privileges were even more eccentric. The Privy Purse, large or small, was income-tax free. There was still the right to use the title of His Highness. This was a matter of great esteem, the more so as it carried with it such amenities as free medical attention for themselves, their families and animals, free water and electricity, exemption from car taxes and gun licences. They could carry their own red state numberplates and fly their flags. There was provision for armed guards for their palaces, or wherever they lived; they could still demand their gun salutes, if they really wanted to. When they passed on to their next *avatar*, they could confidently look forward to full military honours at their funeral.

All this was of course preposterous in a country professing the gospel according to Mrs Gandhi. The idea of a handful of minor Bourbons remaining uncommonly rich from the public funds of a society of grinding poverty was on the face of it odious. The toleration of a few officially ordained Highnesses among five hundred million permanent Lownesses was an absurd anomaly, and India had in all conscience enough of those already.

India, however, is a great place for elusive and enigmatic standards. Indefensible as the Princes' position seemed, they had a sort of case, which they made through an institution called Concord For India, the nearest imaginable thing to a monarchical trade union. Its Intendant-General and Convenor was H. M. Maharaja Sriraj of Dhrangandhra, a highly articulate and business-like ex-ruler and former MP. He had invited me to his office in New Delhi, like that of a busy small-town solicitor, crammed with files and folders and with a telephone to which he had attached the legend: TAPPED. He received me initially with the greatest of well-bred suspicion (he had, reasonably, little to thank the British for, or the Press, or even more specifically me). His doubts markedly diminished with the arrival of Moni, who looks very much more like a Maharani than do most Maharanis.

'Our argument is simply that of legality and justice,' said Dhrangandhra. 'The treaties and compacts were mutually negotiated and agreed, signed by two lawful contracting parties in most solemn circumstances, incorporated in the Constitution, ratified and confirmed by the sovereign body of India. If that doesn't give us a standing in law and honour, what on earth could?'

'But—' said I.

'There is no greater hardship than dishonour. We cherish our self-respect, our *izzat*. The State has a right to exhort co-operation from us, not to extort subservience. The Princes made over their dominions, nearly half of India, for Indian unity; at the time we were praised for our patriotism. Why does that woman – why does the Government now seek our public humiliation?'

That evening we had dinner with the Maharaja of Dewas Junior – a Prince not especially exalted in the hierarchy (his Purse was only 180,000 rupees, roughly £10,000) but much respected and liked by both sides. He surveyed the situation with resigned and ironic detachment.

'The Princes are goners whatever happens, and probably not a bad thing in the long run. I don't know why we old stagers at least couldn't have been allowed just to die off, but that's politics. I'm sixty-six. I haven't got a son; I wouldn't have cost the nation very much for much longer. The money part is pretty irrelevant anyhow. Still, I agree we've got to go.

'Maybe it could have been done more tactfully, more courteously. The Prime Minister asks me up to discuss things; we agree that the decision is irrevocable; she asks me what suggestions I have for the procedure. I am obliged to say: Madam, I haven't got any; if I am told that I am inevitably going to be executed tomorrow it's really of little moment to me whether you use a hemp rope or a gold chain. Please suit yourself; the methodology is of small consequence.'

So it came about that we found ourselves in our hired car driving south. We had negotiated the car from the Tourist Board; it was to cost us, or rather the magazine, an extra fee because it was said to be air-conditioned. We arranged to leave at nine in the morning. After one or two false starts it became necessary to fill up with petrol, then to deliver a couple of parcels, to pay a few courtesy calls on the driver's relations, to enquire about the state of the road. Promptly at eleven we got away.

Our driver was an efficient and well-mannered Sikh with the slightly aloof and cynical demeanour of Sikhs about to leave the Punjab and head south among the blackamoors. He drove very well. The expensive air-conditioning rattled and thundered. Less than twenty miles outside New Delhi it broke down and stopped.

'Mr Singh, what about the air-conditioning?'

'Alas.'

'Mr Singh, please make note that we shall not be paying the surcharge.'

'Not paying surcharge.'

'So long as it is being understood.'

The loss of the air-conditioner's grinding row was indeed something of a relief. From then on it never worked at all.

*

'JAIPUR, the capital of Rajasthan, is what so many people dream that India is and what so many people discover that India is not. Rich in history and tradition, Jaipur has manifold attractions, not least a subtle charm given by the rose-hued buildings....'

Thus the Tourist Guide. In fact Jaipur is a somewhat dull city by day, angularly laid out and built of a pinkish material resembling raspberry ice-cream. Its appearance is at first desolatingly ordinary; only when you realise that its remarkable modernity was laid out by Maharaja Jai Singh II in 1728, when London was sixty per cent a slum, does it begin to seem admirable. By evening it became enchanting.

We were invited by the Rajmata of Jaipur to take photographs of her in the City Palace. 'Or, if you prefer,' she said gaily, 'pictures of the City Palace including me.' The Rajmata, or Queen Mother, is a very striking and vigorous lady indeed.

By a nice irony the leading personalities in the Down-With-Mrs-Gandhi campaign were themselves women. The Rajmatas of Jaipur, Jodhpur, Gwalior and Bikaner, all extremely shrewd and dominant individuals, wielded much political power in Rajasthan and Madhya Pradesh, rather like combinations of dowager duchesses and Barbara Castles. They had not been passing the shrinking years repining over vanished thrones. They were insistently articulate and elected Members of Parliament in the interests of the far-right Swatantra or Janh Sangh parties, militant religious-nationalist groups explicable in our terms only if the Reverend Ian Paisley had somehow been born a Hindu.

Our hostess, HH of Jaipur, had won a fame far outside India; as the reigning Maharani her singularly penetrating good looks and suavely cosmopolitan elegance, not to speak of her riches, had made her very much a part of the international *haut monde*, from which she would from time to time return to India to give the hated Congress Party what for.

'It is imperative', said the Rajmata, posing with accomplished grace among the noble courtyards, 'to contest the influences that are burdening our country. We represent honour, tradition, continuity. Is the light still all right for you? The professional politicians can't do it, or won't do it. Everyone has an axe to grind; I have none, except to represent the people who trusted us for so long. We were the real India. Then let us go in and have some tea.'

The Rajmata of Jaipur was by far the most energetic of the Queen Mothers who, remembering the days of their personal power, far overshadowed their heirs. Her political zeal transcended her Hindu traditionalism; recently widowed, she would ordinarily have been in white mourning and seclusion, but not a bit of it; she would not let Mrs Gandhi off with that. The Rajmata had been a Princess in her own right, from the house of Cooch Behar. She bore with her an agreeable hint of unobtainable French scent.

The sentries still presented arms when they saw her car.

'You have to hand it to her,' said my wife with admiration. That evening we sat in the velvet gloaming of her garden drinking whisky and watching an old film – French, naturally. To the Queen Mother this probably was the real India.

One of the successes of free India was to liberate women from the traditional shadows and, in theory, point them towards the direction of public life. Many achieved it. Every woman who did so was upper- or middle-class; almost all were rich. Consider those who made it; Rajkumari Amrit Kaur, first woman in Nehru's Cabinet; Mrs Vijayalakshmi Pandit, Nehru's sister and first and only woman

President of the UN General Assembly; the poet Sarojini Naidu; the painter Amrita Shergil; Suchetra Kripalani who became Chief Minister of Uttar Pradesh; Dhanvanthi Rama Rau the family planner; Dr Sushila Nayar, once Minister of Health; half a dozen more. All spoke in the voices of Girton, Somerville, Vassar and Smith. There is not and never has been a working-class woman with a function in Indian politics, and it is hard to say when there ever will be. To this day only ten per cent of Indian women can read.

'Give it another fifty or eighty years,' said my wife. 'Do not be impatient.'

Just outside Jaipur lay Amber, the ancient capital, an exquisite place in a stifling gorge. It is possibly one of the half-dozen finest ruins in the world. Through the lovely gardens below the palace ran a stark line of posts and telephone wires. A group of tourists lurched up the great ramp on an elephant, with the insecure uneasiness of all Europeans on elephants. Beside them trotted the guide. 'Here we have now the oldest preserved city in Asia ... in the world....' It was nothing of the kind; nevertheless Amber was a fine city eight centuries ago; even now the abandoned grace of its carving and inlay was sombrely, sadly splendid.

There is one terrible thing in Amber. Within the empty palace is a deserted temple, behind this dark place is a dark shrine for the image of Kali, the dreadful goddess who can be appeased only in blood. She sat hideously, grossly terrifying – black in the face, crooked in the leg, a shrivelled body with pendant breasts, fingers distorted to talons. Her waist is girdled with serpents and around her neck a ring of human skulls. Her teeth are long and the scales of her tongue protrude like the Bes of Egypt, and a single eye stares from her brow. Kali – almost certainly an aboriginal divinity – was absorbed years ago into the Hindu pantheon as the wife of Siva; as his *sakti* or energy she is the potent agency of disease and death. Around Jaipur they thought most highly of her.

Some miles outside Ajmer the road divided; two equal trails forked left and right. The sign: 'To Jodhpur' was clean and newly painted, with the two arrows pointing impartially in both directions. Indian sign-painters do not presume to make decisions for other people. A man herding goats by the roadside said that in all probability the right fork led to Jodhpur, but he had no powerful conviction about it; we suspected that he had never felt obliged to give the matter any serious thought. As it happened his guess was right.

Equivocal signboards are a small part of the agreeable gamble of driving through Rajasthan. The national highways are engineered to pass through three dimensions: length, breadth, and time. They are good enough roads, well surfaced, with adequate filling-stations, convenient food-stalls; they seem limitless. Yet everyone who lives along the route of a national highway still thinks of it as a country lane, a personal convenience, a useful surface on which to doze by day, to spread the drying grain, to perambulate the flocks, to hold wedding feasts and family celebrations. Motor traffic is light indeed, but the old shepherdess will absent-mindedly decide to drive her beasts across the highway precisely at the moment when the car approaches the bush behind which she has been hidden for hours. The solitary cyclist wobbling dreamily on the crown of the road four hundred yards ahead, aroused by the horn, will falter and swerve for half a minute, undecided until the last second whether to weave wildly to left or the right. Two truck drivers, rattling along in opposite directions, will recognise each other as they pass and brake grindingly side by side, wholly blocking the highway while they shrill out their greetings, reaching to fondle each other's forearms, exchanging reminiscences until reluctantly they go on their ways, releasing the road at last. But during that pause the road, apparently running through an uninhabited desert, has become miraculously peopled with villagers crowding around the car to chat, to sell nuts or mangoes, to ask where you are from and where you are going, to beg, or to stare. It takes a long time for the stranger in village India to understand that the gatherings around a car, peering and pointing and giggling and touching and chattering unintelligibly, are being neither rude nor moronic, but curious in a strangely innocent way.

Mile after mile, hour after hour. There is a sense of endlessness on the Indian road that you do not get even on the interminable plains of the American Middle West — the vast latitudinal highways of Nebraska and the Dakotas are longer, and wider, and better, and above all straighter, but they lead from one indistinguishably semi-civilised place to another; the United States is one solid mass-produced society to an extent India can never be; in India one is not driving through a country but a continent, the invisible frontiers here are truly ethnic dividing-lines — here the beards will be cut otherwise, the saris tied differently, the languages incomprehensible to each other three hundred miles apart. Rajasthan was and always will be more Indian than anywhere else, if only because it never was anything else; this had never technically been British India at all.

Mr Singh drove us well, with a practised indifference to all around him, good or bad. It was, he implied by his contemptuous skimming of bullock-carts and sudden roarings on the horn, no more his country than ours; this was not Sikh territory, not the well-managed husbandry of the Punjab. And indeed it was not, yet it was a thousand times better than when last I had seen it – already long stretches of the arid Rajasthan wilderness had become green and at least embryonically fertile, haystacks like little onion-domes of mosques; the desert was beginning to surrender. Moni had not seen these plains for even longer than I; she continually called to point out improbable patches of cultivation which only an Indian would have observed.

Now the clothes of the peasant women were gay, bright vermilions and saffron, gorgeous tattered colours unknown in the North. Far ahead of the car would appear a small crowd of them spread all over the highway. Mr Singh would lean on the horn. Nobody would pay the least attention. The car hurtled on; the crowd would scatter casually, almost absent-mindedly, as though the idea of dispersing had occurred to them spontaneously and by some sort of fortuitous inspiration. Refusing to slow down in the least we would miss several of them by millimetres, without for a moment interrupting anyone's conversation. Seconds after we had swept on our way they were again all over the road; just as they had been unaware of their peril they gave no thanks for their escape.

An hour later we drew up at the roadside where a boy was selling tender coconuts, which once I used to love immoderately. They were piled in a great pile from the tree like an enormous bunch of brown grapes. The boy detached a couple and prepared them in the fashion that always reminded me of a professional West End oyster-opener: half a dozen swift chops from the machete marginally missed his fingertips, and there was the oval cup opened at the top like a boiled egg, dripping with the cool and delicate milk, the most refreshing liquid in nature. The boy gave us a spoon-shaped fragment of shell with which to scoop the transparent rubbery meat of the nut. What an economy: cup, drink, food and implement all within one shell.

It was late when we reached Jodhpur. Here, like almost everywhere else, the former ruler (or perhaps his administrators, since himself was still a simple youth from Oxford) was in the process of turning his palace into an hotel. The process was obviously far from completed. The hotel wing was in total darkness and seemingly permanently uninhabited. Much hooting and hallooing and peering around in back quarters finally produced a bemused and drowsy watchman, uneasy at being roused, probably for the first time in his career, from a deep and refreshing night's work. He was clearly disposed to wash his hands of the whole business, but by this time our importunities had awakened several more blanketed colleagues, who pottered about in an aimless anxiety winding up their headcloths.

We were admitted at last into the embryo hotel, once the royal guest-quarters. It suggested a very big secondhand seaside boarding-house. Our room, fitfully lit by two forty-watt bulbs, was apparently furnished by the Public Works Department with odds and ends left over from a government hostel. There was great talk in princely circles of cashing in on history and attracting American tourists to these now-public palaces, and though much enterprising work was going on elsewhere in Rajasthan, as we were to find out, it had got off to a very dismal start here. The first thing that fell off was the wardrobe door. The shower was stained with rust. In the deep basement was a cavernous and sepulchral swimming-pool, grey and menacing, like a crocodile-tank in a horror film.... The hotel seemed to have surrendered before it had given itself a chance. No one else was staying there except a young British couple of inscrutable background in some way associated with an educational foundation. We were all summoned to a truly dreadful dinner in what seemed to be a converted spare bedroom, served by a butler with an air of settled melancholy. He was, it seemed, unable to find a drink, everything was locked up.... It was an unpropitious evening.

The next day was not lightened by the onset of forebodings within my inside. I had long been more or less immunised against the more obvious tropical disturbances, or as far as anyone could be; there were such a multitude of things one could suffer from quite apart from the major horrors. The guts-ache came in so many sneaking shapes: amoebiasis, bacillary dysentery, lambliasis: they all came down to the same squalid thing. One carried specifics around and dosed oneself when one remembered: sodas and bromides and tablets of iodochlorhydroxyquinoline, and some stuff in a tube called, mind-bendingly: stearylaminophenyltrimethylammoniumsulphomethylate. They made no difference; sooner or later your number came up, and you got it, always where you needed it least.

It is my experience, since we are on this morbid consideration, that misfortune of this nature always struck at a place where Indian technology was at its more perverse: where the toilet-roll fitting was always just out of reach of the lavatory seat. This is as though India, obliged and indeed eager to come to terms with the wholly alien concepts of the tourist, must always reserve the right to modify them just a bit, to show at the same time their mastery of these things and their rejection of them. Lavatory-paper is a concept ancestrally repugnant to Indians in their personal life; nevertheless for the visitor it is a requirement always desirable and sometimes downright imperative. Therefore it must be available, but only *just* available.... Enough is enough. The malady cured itself, as it always does, but I did not see Jodhpur at my best.

The young Maharaja had returned, and he was kind enough to ask us to take the evening meal with him, his sister and the Rajmata. Indian radicals were wont to joke about Jodhpur as a decadent Western hippy, back after his years of adolescence in Oxford just in time to see his divine inheritance slip down the drain. He was indeed a somewhat camp young man, but gentle and courteous withal, and clearly in a state of total bewilderment at the nature of the political conflict that enveloped him. He admitted that he found the palace – a classic piece of nondescript ostentation, built by the Raj in 1929 in the likeness of the late Wembley Exhibition and at a reputed cost of seven million pounds – unhomely in comparison with his mod life in England. His mother, the powerful Rajmata, insisted upon his dynastic obligations, and he had just submitted almost diffidently to the dharshans with his ex-subjects, the reverences and the kissing of his feet. 'They seem to love us,' he said. 'I don't know; I wish I could do more for them.'

During the meal an odd thing became apparent: while one group of bearers was serving us, another individual bearer was serving His Highness. What was more, His Highness was clearly getting a better class of dinner. One did not have to be envious to see that while we were getting cold and listless *chappatis* and *dhal* HH was getting aromatic partridge; what was more, one perceived outside in the corridor a servant fanning a charcoal brazier on which he was making piping-hot *phulkas* with which the young man was steadily being plied, though none came our way. When the meal was over, we were offered Indian whisky. HH was given Scotch. It seemed an odd acceptance by a rich young man brought up in conventions of England and Oxford; he appeared to be as unaware of the anomaly as he was of everything else.

Next day we headed towards Udaipur, where everything was going to be all right.

Just outside the Jain temple at Ranakhpur we picked up a hitch-hiker, a young man sitting by the roadside with a smile of such confident sweetness it could not be resisted. He carried a satchel over his shoulder.

'Where do you want to go?'

'To the next village. I am the postman.'

'Do you always deliver the mail this way, getting the lifts?'

'Oh yes. Saving walk.'

The village was seven miles along the road. We dropped the postman with expressions of mutual pleasure.

'How will you get back?'

'Get lift. Get bus. Maybe stay.'

'What about the mail?'

He laughed happily. 'Mail? I am postman!'

I felt we had made our small contribution to the Indian communications system.

Once we stopped at a roadside tea-house; the proprietor had contrived it from odd boards and sheets of galvinised iron, a brazier within, around it tables with oilcloth covers, a floor of stamped mud. Half a dozen country customers sat watchfully around; our arrival stopped their conversation. After a while I had a feeling like that of Kafka's 'K' in *The Castle*, surrounded by the peasants in the anonymous Inn: 'He turned to look at them and found that they, too, were looking at him. When he saw them sitting like that, however, each man in his own place, not speaking to one another and without any apparent mutual understanding, united only by the fact that they were all gazing at him, he concluded that it was not out of malice that they pursued him, perhaps they really wanted something from him and were only incapable of expressing it;

if not that it might be pure childishness, which seemed to be in fashion. . . .'

I decided that it was not my European clothes which interested them, nor yet Moni's sari, but the puzzling fact that we were together; it was the relationship that held their attention. As soon as we left they would talk about it for hours.

The plains were a dusty throb of heat. I weary very quickly of long motor tours, even when conducted with the lordly mastery of a Mr Singh. He drove with the practised skill of a professional knife-thrower; the art was to aim as nearly as possible to everything without actually hitting it. The only occasions on which he permitted the flicker of a smile to cross his bearded lips were when some day-dreaming pedestrian would be obliged to dive for his life behind a tree or into a doorway.

It was with relief that we saw below us the hill-ringed cool expanse of the lake at Udaipur.

Like many of the shrewder Princes coming to terms with the new times, the Maharana of Udaipur was turning his property into hotels. His Lake Palace was different in that at once I knew it – as a lifelong denizen and victim of hotels – to be one of the pleasantest I had ever known. It occupied the whole area of a little island in the Pichola Lake. Its age was indeterminate; it had been modernised with skill and taste. To our parched and fatigued spirits the lake on which it seemed to float, the omnipresent water, was a vast refreshment. There we were relaxed and happy.

But on the first night I was still so wound up I could not sleep. I sat up at the wide window looking over the hills. The water of the lake lapped ten feet below the window; it was like glowing pewter. The spectacle framed in that window was of a splendour so perfect it could have been a mise-en-scéne. The moon was at the full, or almost;

it hung in that velvet sky like a brilliant Chinese lamp, illuminating the mountains in a sequence of receding planes: grey into black into sable, arranged in composition so preposterously romantic and stylised that any conceivable reproduction of it would have had to be rejected as an outrageous idealisation. At the summit of the nearest ridge stood the tiny form of the Maharana's Monsoon Palace, by day a vague shape hardly distinguishable from the mass of the surrounding peaks, but now in this vivid moonlight a stark and almost iridescent white, the apotheosis of the fairy-tale castle. While I watched, the huge disc of the moon passed briefly behind it and the flowing white of the hilltop palace turned to silhouette. At one moment the fluttering shapes of the fruit-bats cut across the circle of the moon, in the final touch of Disneyland magic.

In the morning I awoke hearing the sound of a faraway tattoo of drums. I thought it to be the beginning of a festival on the mainland. In fact the drumming came from an immense line of washermen crouched on the dhobighats beside the lake, thumping out the laundry against the stones. This gentle rhythm opened every day. It was taken up by the doves' continual murmuring grumble of remonstrance, and the whirr as they took off on their rattling wings. Pigeons are the only real cosmopolitans of the world. There may be differences between the peasant birds and the gross urban pigeons of London, Venice, Allahabad or Glasgow, but I cannot discern them; they all wear the same clerical uniform and do the same selfish things. Only once do I remember seeing them put to human use: in Peking, where the Chinese strapped little flutes to them and filled the air with inexplicable windy music.

In this lovely place the days passed with a splendidly unfamiliar aimlessness. We took a boat and drifted across

the lake to the other island on which stood the Jag Mandir
Palace, a building of if anything even greater charm,
which the Maharana – by now in partnership with the
huge Parsi commercial house of Tata – was turning into
yet another hotel. Clearly someone of taste was at work in
Udaipur. Indian sumptuous architecture, once so baroque
and magnificent, had of late tended to vary between the
stylistic idioms of the discothèque and the railway-station
waiting-room. Even the most enthusiastic Edgware-Road-
Orientaliser would have had difficulty spoiling the decent
proportions of these places and nor, so far, had they
tried.

From the main platform of the palace a flight of stone
steps dropped into the lake. On the topmost step a large
turtle was taking its ease in the sun; it must have been
three feet long and weighed many pounds. I have a particular fondness for turtles and tortoises, indeed the whole
family Testudinidae, and I was impelled to stop the boat's
slow drift and consider the question of how this turtle in
question had physically contrived to climb the steep stone
stairs to the broad platform at their top, since the many
qualities of the turtle race do not include agility or (as
I know from peculiar experience) the ability to negotiate
even the smallest steps. As I pondered this beguiling mys-
ery the turtle awoke with a start, gazed stonily about,
levered itself to the platform's edge, and tobogganed down
the slippery stairway into the lake, exactly in the manner
of a lifeboat launching itself onto the sea. This experience
gave me the greatest pleasure.

As the evening fell the air became populated with a
new traffic. A large colony of parakeets lived, it seemed,
in various crannies of the old Jag Mandir palace, but spent
their days foraging ashore on the mainland, commuting
back and forth with the coming and ending of the day.
The homeward rush-hour had now begun, and the para-

keets streamed homeward across the lake in a disciplined cloud of whirring wings.

But as the birds returned to sleep the bats awoke. In a grove of big mango-trees by the mainland water's edge, by the City Palace, there dwelt a community of fruit-bats, the largest I had ever seen, creatures the size of cats, in an enormous abundance. All day they slumbered hanging upside-down among the branches in strange festoons like dangling furry fruit. As the sun went down they stirred and dropped into the air, one at a time, by dozens, by scores, by hundreds, wheeling and drifting over the lake on their two-foot leather wingspread, erratic and dark and silent against the sky like ashes blown from a great bonfire. A big bat in flight, scouring the evening for food, is an eerie and magical sight; hundreds of them together is almost Wagnerian. I could have watched this for hours, but Moni decided that the bats were unsupportably sinister, as indeed they were, which was what I liked about them. Moni and I share most opinions, but not on zoology; reptiles leave her cold and bats repel her. I do not think it is a wholly Indian flaw; I have observed these prejudices elsewhere.

After dinner that night they brought over to entertain us a little travelling puppet-theatre of the Rajasthan tradition – a tiny company, four of a peasant family. It was simple, crude, witty, and delightful. While the husband manipulated the marionettes the wife intoned and sang the narrative; the three-year-old daughter sat beside her holding the baby. The baby had been born just twenty days before.

All these serenities were so different from all I had had of India before. In twenty-five years of erratic Indian experience I had never before known this sort of self-indulgence; now for a week I was a tourist.

Tourists, of course, were exactly what the hotel was for.

Agreeable though it was, the island was limiting. Next day as the washermen were drumming out their morning tattoo on the dhobi-ghat we boated ashore to Udaipur. It had still not surrendered to being an annexe of the posh hotel; Udaipur was still at that time just a little too far off the track to have touristified itself. We walked in a happily pointless way through streets with no billboards, no posters, no advertisements for laxatives or sparking-plugs, no piped music. This Indian town was still – so far – an Indian town. Could that possibly have had anything to do with Princely rule?

We were asked for drinks by the Maharana in the City Palace. Maharana is a subtle improvement on Maharaja, a delicate elevation in rank, befitting the man who claimed to be the heir to the longest-established dynasty in the world. For some reason, allegedly an old curse, the succession has rarely gone to a direct son; the present Maharana himself had been adopted. His name, for the record, was HH Hindua Maharajadhiraja Maharana Sri Bhagwat-Singhji Bahadur. He was quiet and courteous and earnest; he seemed too modest for the surroundings of the City Palace. We sat on the terrace of this imposing establishment, surveying this incomparable prospect of lake and hills; bearers produced our whiskies with almost theatrical deference; here and there secretaries and ADCs loitered watchfully; loitering watchfully was their job. It was difficult to feel that even in the changed circumstances much serious inconvenience had befallen His Highness, yet his argument conveyed a sense of intangible loss.

'A question of keeping faith. For that lady to say that the Privy Purses and privileges are incongruous in the concept of democracy is to bely the Constitution itself, which established democracy in India *and* enshrined our rights. If subsidising the Princes is suddenly undemocratic now, why wasn't it in 1947 when the nation was made, with us part of it? Weren't Gandhi and Nehru and Patel and the rest of them supposed to be democrats?

'In any case the Purses aren't *grants*, like pensions. They were what we retained from what was ours when we renounced everything else. . . .

'I offered to put my Privy Purse into a Foundation, long before this row began. We're ready to negotiate everything – Purses, privileges, possessions, anything. But it should be done with decorum. She ought to have left us our dignity. We have, after all, nothing else left. . . .'

There was the handsome garden, the scores of lavish rooms, the army of servants, the acres of land, the assortment of Palaces.

'You think me selfish. But it is for the people. . . .

'A little while ago I walked sixteen miles on foot to the shrine of my tutelary deity for puja. They followed, twenty thousand came along.'

There was an air of unreality, a sense of wildly mixed-up values, of cosmic triviality. Now the Maharana, last of a ruling line of fourteen hundred unbroken years, turning his palaces into hotels, trusts, museums, anything.

'I am grateful to you for coming. Have you seen the fountain gardens?'

The fountain gardens downtown were now run by the Public Works Department. We paid a rupee each and were admitted. No fountains were playing. After a time an official appeared. He went round the gardens turning on each jet with a turncock. He allowed each jet to splutter and come to life for a moment, then turned it off and moved to the next.

Had I had the eloquence, I would have liked to have suggested to this custodian that the whole point of a fountain garden is that its fountains should play, at random, prodigally, wastefully pretty. The city was, after all, almost made of water. But this dreary official, plodding round

135

turning the fountains on and off like the late President Johnson with the White House light-switches, was doing no more than he was bidden. There was none but us to watch the fountains anyhow.

*

It was one of the endless discussions in the Club; so quickly they turn into lectures.

'We can't just wish away the British occupation, however much we'd like to; everywhere you look it's still there. What we can do – and we do it all the time – is offload all our shortcomings and inadequacies on British history. This is indispensable to the Indian character. We don't do it with the same conviction as we used to, because it's beginning to look a bit silly after twenty-five years; still it's instinctive to pass the buck.

'All the same we're wholly ambivalent about the Raj. We're supposed to thank the British for giving us a public service and a system of law and at least a kind of unity. What we should be thanking them for is giving us their language, simply because it gave us access to the literature of dissatisfaction and revolt, which we simply never thought of producing for ourselves. Almost all literate Indians were exposed at some time or other to J. S. Mill and the rest of them. Obviously the only object the British had in educating us was to make us more useful clerks and babus, but as it turned out they couldn't do that without handing over the instruments of their own ultimate abolition. Frankly I don't see how they could have avoided it.

'We used our own methodology, to be sure, but the libertarian ideas were theirs, after all, and because the British ruling class is so bloody dumb they drummed this stuff into us with their exams and so on without knowing what the hell they were doing. It always seemed odd to me that your Churchill, for example, who lived on the same sort of pretentious hollow rhetoric as we do, was so taken aback and outraged by the Indian intellectual rebellion. Come to think of it, maybe he wasn't very clever at all, just brilliant.

'No, what we have against the British is that they undermined our sense of personal history – probably by accident, the way they do everything. Extraordinary how a few thousand Anglo-Saxon expatriates could brainwash millions of Indians. They encouraged us to live in the past romantically and the future competitively, so we became indifferent to our present. That wasn't difficult, of course, with the Hindu character. Our history is just a sort of myth-worship, anyhow.

'The real cruelty was that Britain robbed us of our revolution. They conned us out of our national revolution of violence, so we lost the utopian momentum of real rebellion. Since we never had that, we coasted along, we compromised. All of a sudden in 1947 we found we actually owned our own present, and we were so uneasy about it we propped up a wonderful new idea on old institutions. We inherited a bureaucracy far more English than Indian – worse, we embraced it, we cherished it, we multiplied and embellished it; to every one of its pompous bumbling ineptitudes we added more, for every opportunity for graft and nepotism we provided yet better and more crafty ones. The system was paralysed with precedents, so every year we accreted new ones. The British bequeathed us a hierarchical machinery – but, boy, when it comes to hierarchical institutions nobody can teach India anything. Today our bureaucracy is twenty times more bureaucratic, our snobberies more snobbish, our deference to the chain of command more cringing and decorous, our worship of paper more entrenched. The British created our regiments of minor ill-paid babus in the image of the Dickensian clerk and there he remains, enshrining the second-rate, terrified of decisions, passing responsibility upwards from hand to hand until it gets lost in the clouds of unseen authority.

'We have no real industrialists, only speculators. We invent nothing, since it is easier to copy, and what we copy we usually demean or falsify....'

Then the passion fades suddenly away, the phrases stop, the eyes cloud over. 'Bearer, tea.'

Witness the arrival of the local politician at any smallish town. The reception committee, dozens strong, will have long assembled at the airport, the garlands ready, the phrases prepared. The politician will appear, a small furtive man, or a large glossy man some distance behind his own stomach; in either case he knows his power. The disciples surround him, pressing their palms in greeting; everyone smiles with a sort of desperation; he does not. He acknowledges the scene through lifeless eyes, pacing through the press of acolytes without pause into the eagerly opened door of his car; the wildly bobbing faces against the window. The blank dull eyes have noted everyone: the small man, the little trader, the petty official, each with his own preoccupation – and he has already selected those for consideration on the morrow, when the procession for favours arrives at his threshold: the licence for this or for that, the amelioration of some penalty or reduction of a fine, a tax concession, a permission, a letter of recommendation, a *chitthi* to authority. He will oblige those who may later advantage him, he will reject those who have nothing to offer, most he will send empty away until such time as they can find his price. He himself is a small man, a petty man; in the Centre he himself will be found among the obsequious and the supplicants, but here at his roots he is of importance and the nearest thing to power, and this is why he is in politics at all: the brief period of patronage, and the only point in patronage is profit.

Corruption in India is almost as leaden a cliché as hunger. It is sanctified by the oldest of traditions: it is denied by nobody, indeed the totality and pervasiveness of Indian corruption is almost a matter of national pride: just as India's droughts are the driest, her famines the most cruel, her over-population the most uncontrollable, so are all the aspects of Indian corruption and bribery the most wholly widespread and spectacular.

Public or private venality is no longer even a serious talking-point in India any more than is the weather in England. There can be no earthly way of establishing its extent. It is just possible, indeed, that it is not as enormous as is generally supposed, but this of course is of less importance than that its enormity is generally supposed and accepted, with a consequent national cynicism most melancholy in a nation forever proclaiming itself as a socialist democracy. The process is therefore acknowledged and ratified; it is ordained that every official can be bribed, every commodity can be adulterated, every scarcity can be exploited, every contract can be fiddled, every privilege can be bought, every examination can be wangled, every bureaucrat must be paid not just to expedite the application-form but specifically not to obstruct it. It is almost as though the whole concept of public morality had been gear-shifted into another dimension, with another norm. The figures of tax-evasion are astronomical: something like a hundred and fifty million pounds are lost to the revenue every year; endless Reports and Commissions have made it clear to a weary public who, if they are literate enough to read them, are themselves too involved to worry, let alone protest.

I suppose it could be argued that India – that tiny part of India that is occupied in business and affairs, both great and small – is probably the world's most dishonest country, if we are to accept the normally hypocritical Puritan standards of the West. That is probably an abstract fact; the truth is as perhaps otherwise : that without bribery Indian commerce and industry would be suffocated with controls and obstructions, and the national product would eventually become nothing but enormous warehouses full of files.

'What then is the businessman to do?' You hear it on all sides at parties, on golf-courses. 'We are not in England. When we die no government will look after our family; we get no free medicines, free schools, pensions.... Do I want my widow to sleep on the streets? Do I want my children to beg for their rice? I must make at least a lakh each dowry for my daughters to persuade anyone to marry them. Let the Government show the slightest sense of social responsibility for *anyone* but themselves and maybe things will change : why should I pay taxes to support these bloody rich Socialists in luxury?'

There was something in what they said. India has more than 500 Ministers – more than any other country in the world : 55 at the Centre and more than 455 in the States of the Union. They are all pledged to Gandhian austerity. A Union Minister draws a gross income, including legal perquisites, of about 37,500 rupees a month, rather more than £2,000, which is to say some 800 times the income of the All-Indian average. They live in opulent houses – the market rent on a Ministerial bungalow in New Delhi is as a rule between 2,000 and 5,000 rupees a month; their tax is negligible; their medical and travel facilities are paid out of public funds. From these surroundings they

proclaim their socialism, they inveigh against the capital-
ists, fiddlers and tycoons. One would mind less about their
life-style did they not protest that they represent the desti-
tute and needy, were they not the Government that *itself*
agrees that 200 million Indians live, or try to live, below
any humanly accepted poverty datum-line – were they not,
in short, the democratic administration of the poorest
nation on earth?

How did China manage it and India fail?

The answer cannot be Communism, if only because I
do not know if anyone any longer knows what Communism is. In India it is wildly fragmented, and the rival sects
spend more time denouncing each other's heresies than
those of the enemy.

I suppose in a way I could understand this.

Life was forever being interrupted by flashbacks.

I had once been a war correspondent in the first major
anti-Red confrontation, in Korea. It was to my mind a very
unwholesome situation, not to say totally disagreeable
from every point of view, and it came about in the end
that I was obliged to find grave fault with the behaviour
of all sides, not just that of our foes the Commie-dogs but
also that of the unpleasant little tyrant the late President
Synghman Rhee, who at this time occupied the role of
our gallant South Korean ally, and who was taking the
opportunity of the war to engage in some freelance butch-
ery of his own. This, needless to say, was not a popular
attitude to take up. Indeed by and by it brought about a
dire crisis in the journal for which I was then happily working, the ever-regretted *Picture Post*, and in effect finally
destroyed it. I have described the episode at interminable
length before in another book, and there is no need to
exhume it again.

Years later, in my search for employment, my professional safari through the jungles of Fleet Street, I spent a

while in the service of the *Daily Mirror*. It was a brief interlude but helpful for me, since I was allowed to share a room with William Connor, the celebrated columnist Cassandra, of the terse and biting tongue. He was (as indeed most of my colleagues have always been) extremely kind to me, and made this unfamiliar *Mirror* environment a decent haven for a while.

There came a day when the *Mirror*, understandably deciding that the only value they could get out of me was a measure of hindsight and experience, thought it a good idea for me to go back to Korea, now that the shot and shell had abated. This commission greatly appealed to me, and I put the familiar old machinery into gear for such a move.

I checked and renewed my inoculations (obtaining one from an absent-minded airline doctor which was later found to read: 'Mr J. Cholera has been immunised against Cameron'). At the War Office Major Flood and Captain Brookes assured me there should be no trouble about my immediate accreditation, since I already held my valid United Nations card. I got my Japanese entry visa from the Japanese, my transit visa from the Burmese. I signed for my passage to Tokyo.

The next day Colonel Hobbs at the War Office rang Bill Connor, in some embarrassment, to say that Intelligence, whoever they were, had raised an objection to me. They would provide no reason. The Colonel was kind enough to say he could not imagine what it could be. Nor could I, nor could anyone. I could not believe that causing offence to the now-discredited Synghman Rhee could be a reason for the British Army's displeasure. The Americans possibly, but I was not seeking American auspices. I argued that a matter of principle was involved, and I put this to the Editor of the newspaper, the late Bish Bolam, who spontaneously and generously offered me his full blanket support, accepting that the whole affair was some dotty misunderstanding.

Next day Bill Connor went to see Colonel Hobbs. He returned to say gruffly that they would accredit him, if he wanted to go, but not me.

The matter built up into absurdity. The Editor went to see Anthony Head, the War Minister.

The late Bish Bolam was a kind man too. He called me in and said that the War Office's rejection of me was because of 'Communist associations, more than can be explained professionally'.

So that was it; it was almost a relief to realise its triviality. Those daft days of 1939 – or was it 1940, and were they so daft? – those joyless little conclaves of the Socialist Study Group in the bleak room over the Fleet Street pub where, for a few weeks, we played with the notion of reforming society, since nobody else seemed to be giving much thought to it. It took an effort of memory to recall: the earnest exchange of quotations over the cracked teacups, the harsh heated lectures from the old hands of the real Party, contemptuous of our suspected frivolity; the half-crown subs for the hire of the room; the sense of frustrated drama. . . . Until by and by it became too numbingly boring, and until the bombs began to fall all around and a sort of reality crashed in on our play-acting.

That was it: it had lasted but a week or two, but presumably it had gone on someone's file. Intelligence had been more diligent with me than they had been later with Philby or Maclean or Burgess or Blake.

Communism always seemed to me to be an admirable religion, for those who needed religion; its incantations had a sort of sacerdotal character. It also seemed that it could well be a good social system too, though I could not see that anyone had ever tried it. I have been to every People's Democracy in the world, where I found things to admire and to detest in almost equal measure. I have no real dogma about it. The debate on the subject seems to me to have wandered so far from the course; it is sterile and exasperating.

Was I a Communist? I suppose I was, for a week or two, some thirty-odd years ago, although I cannot remember ever having been given anything to establish it, nor was I aware of joining anything, other than our earnest little quorum over the pub. Until that eerie day in Cassandra's office I had forgotten the interlude; it still seems of far less importance than so much that happened since, including a few wars. The years had established that whatever I was it was not a Party man, of any Party, least of all the one that had liberated Prague.

If I were a Chinese I would most certainly be a Communist. If I were a Czech I would certainly not be. And if I were an Indian?

As far as I know there has never been any really Indian thinking on Communism. From the first establishment of the CPI in 1920 it followed the international line in its formation, or adoption, of ideology and strategy, its aims conditioned by the aims and requirements of an exterior international movement without any detectable variant for Indian needs. It is hard to see how it could have been otherwise. There is surely no earthly way of reconciling Marxist–Leninist principles with a society so entrenched in the hierarchical values of caste, and whatever one feels about it there can be no denying that India is such a society, and will be such a society for a long time to come. That seems to me to be the essential factor, and why I cannot believe that India will find the Chinese answer. The Indian Communists of both camps, identifying with either Peking or Moscow, scorn this facile argument, and they may be right.

'No man has done more physical harm to the poor of

the world than Mahatma Gandhi.' Thus John Gerassi, in *Towards Revolution*.

'He may or may not have taught them how to be happy in poverty, but in the material world he hated so ferociously he influenced millions to accept as "good" misery, suffering, disease, exploitation ... condemned all material progress.... Gandhi may have helped save their souls – no mortal can testify to that – but he certainly did strengthen their oppressors. In brute material terms he was an accomplice – in fact, a conspirator – to the murder of millions of children whose parents to this day continue to believe that if they accept their "fate", their place in the world, their own souls will be freed.... And since a revolutionary is he who knows that "one's place" is determined by man and guns and not gods, it is little wonder that so few revolutionaries exist among India's teeming millions.'

All this it must be admitted is the truth, or a sort of truth – or perhaps the kind of fact that obscures the truth. I am far from sure that 'one's place' is determined either by guns or by gods; I do not personally, as they say, use either of them. I have grown accustomed to being startled, even sentimentally shocked, by the vilification and contempt heaped on Gandhi by the younger zealots of the left. Not many years ago I saw something that I could scarcely believe: the burning of Gandhi in effigy in a Calcutta street.

They are right: Gandhi would have made a rotten Party man. While India was celebrating the Independence he had worked his life for Gandhi was walking the roads of rioting Bengal, trying to intercede with the desperate and reassure the fear-stricken. He had to be butchered to stop him becoming the conscience of India. He would indeed have been a terrible embarrassment today.

Sooner or later every Indian, except the most cynical, feels obliged to extricate himself from an argument by saying that, at least, the Indians stem from an immemorial past, that they were a civilised and cultivated people when most Europeans were hopping round the tribal tree. The legend that the Indian civilisation antedates all others is a received truth. Respectful visitors accept it as eagerly as Indians promote it, and indeed never fail to make reference to it on occasions like Rotary Club luncheons.

I accept this agreeable doctrine as easily as everyone else, but the fact of the matter seems to be that no authority can claim to know much about it at all. It is established that the history of Hindustan began when the tribal Aryans descended from central Asia on the northern plains. It is accepted that they stayed a long time, but since they built of mud and wattle and thatch, raised no recognisable tombs nor monuments, and were illiterate the evidence of themselves that they left behind was meagre to say the least, and consisted mainly of a verbal canon of devotional songs, developed before writing, which was later presented in a text and called the Rig-Veda. (Even this cannot be correctly spelled in our terms; the purists insist on Rg-Vehda.) Hindus, and especially Brahmins, are greatly awed by the Rig-Veda, even those who have barely read a line of it, much as many a devout Marxist would be hard put to claim he had actually read *Das Kapital*.

A patriotic Indian usually cites this Rig-Veda as proof of the incalculable antiquity of his culture, though even the most diligent scholars cannot fix a conjectural date on it earlier than 1500 BC, which is a thousand years after the blossoming of the Sumerian civilisation. Nevertheless, a loyal Indian will insist that its incantations and poesies mark the absolute dawn of human achievement.

A study of this mysterious matter – or better still a discussion with one of the really opaque Hindu schoolmen – produces some enchanting word-games. I had dabbled for a long time in the shallows of this business; with my new

Indian connection I began to try harder. One could have tried forever.

The Nasadiyasukta mantra defines the genesis of the world 'from an inscrutable darkness, neither existent nor non-existent, one that breathed without afflation, and beyond it nothing'. It is not a principle that could be described as precise. Yet the words poured out, on and on. After the Vedas came the Brahmanas and the Upanishads which according to these Hindus scholiasts constitute the gnostic part of the Vedas, and the paravidhya superior science concerning the cessation of volition and action and extrication from metempsychosis, the hyperphysical concept of totality....

I have listened to Brahmin gurus, both true and bogus, going on forever in this impenetrable vein, propounding this incomprehensible consideration until a drowsy numbness pained the senses almost to the point of anaesthesia. I once conducted an interview, for the purposes of a film called *The Road To Kingdom Come*, with a highly distinguished Brahmin swami in a Delhi rose-garden of singular charm. With a relentless fluency and walking round and round, he articulated his interlocking principles in a terminology so convoluted and obscure that I could take in nothing except that his perambulations fell into the famous ever-decreasing circles, round and round and round, until we were rotating as it were on our own axis, when I have to say that a combination of bewilderment and vertigo caused me to fall semi-conscious to the scented soil muttering for mercy.

However, it was long ago in my life as a simple reporter that I decided that facts must never get in the way of the truth, and I persisted. The *facts*, then, would seem to be that if we take 1500 BC as a starting-point of the cultivation which for loyal Indians marks the birth of human purpose (or, for that matter, non-purpose) then even they have to admit that a thousand years then passed with nothing that a geologist or archaeologist for example could claim as history – no statuary, no temples, no memorials. The words endure, to be sure, expressing messages of great profundity and beauty, but uttered only by legendary figures, myths, gods, unreachable psalmists. No recognisably human figures emerge at all. There are summits of Sanskrit literature, but there is no history, nor formal tragedy, no Sophocles, no Herodotus, no Euripides. It makes very tough going.

I suppose most Westerners know more of the *Bhagavad Gita* than of any other Asian work. This is not surprising because it is a masterpiece, and furthermore of dimensions reasonable enough to be put up in innumerable limp-leather pocket volumes resembling *Omar Khayyam*, and on a certain level it can be readily absorbed. The *Bhagavad Gita* had no Fitzgerald, unfortunately, and some of its translations give it a form of daunting banality. There is a disastrous relationship between Sanskrit and European languages that drives what must have been sublime writing into what can only be called Californian-Guru-talk, full of 'supreme spirit', 'deep Infinite', 'transcendental unity'.

It is nevertheless, or can be, a quite tormenting allegory, without question one of the great argumentative poems of the world. In the setting of an ancient dynastic war Arjuna and his charioteer face an enemy largely composed of old friends and relations of his boyhood. Arjuna – who is presented as a sort of athletic staff officer, neither intellectual nor wholly foolish, the like of which one has met in wars throughout the world – asks counsel of his charioteer, who is also as it happens the god Krishna. It is as though a Sandhurst battalion commander should have discovered that his jeep is being driven by St Francis of Assisi. This is very fine indeed.

The soldier asks for a definition of the nature of action. He is told: that which is engaged upon for rewards of wealth or the applause of others; or a better kind, which is for no rewards, indifferent both to gain and to the opinions of anyone else. In the better case, all rules and codes of right and wrong are forgotten. In short, the god Krishna is proposing a moral anarchy, and what is interesting is that every decent and devout Indian who reads this poem believes its message to be otherwise.

What Krishna insists is that the wise man knows there is no *reason* for any positive action other than that it proves he is not tied to action; if the results of his action appear to others to be good, and generous, it is only because that is far less troublesome than to be bad. The easiest thing is love. But of whom? 'Why,' says Krishna, 'of me. I am all there is.'

I do not find this the simplest of conundrums, but I think it has some meaning, greater or smaller, for every Indian in the world. However sophisticated, educated, industrialised, rich, poor, self-indulgent, corrupt, crooked or pitiful he may be there comes this occasional imperative impulse to kill the self, to abolish the self – not necessarily for any moral or spiritual reason but from the recurrent need to re-establish the Indian character. Thus any Indian, in conversation with a Westerner, will respond eagerly and intelligently – up to the moment when, for reasons he can never understand, he abandons you. His eyes withdraw; he nods and smiles but he no longer looks; he answers and he no longer hears; he maintains the courtesy of oblivion. This could explain how in company cultivated Indians can allow themselves to be engaged in long party-conversation of such suffocating emptiness: they are basically elsewhere.

Now that I had become tentatively, and putatively, and diffidently, a small part of India, the literature was quite alarming. The philosopher-poets of the Upanishads broke every rule of logical positivism that my Scottish Christian fathers upheld. (Although my grandfather, son of a small Highland farmer, taught himself both Sanskrit and Hebrew, and nevertheless became a Presbyterian minister; it would have been salutary to have been properly acquainted with such a sternly devout heretic.)

The old teachers' doctrine centred round the *atman* – a portmanteau concept that means, I suppose, the 'soul'. Or perhaps rather the Freudian definition of self, divided into Ego, Id, Super-Ego. The old Indians demanded as a first principle that you got rid of your Id, your seat of human appetites. If you could control them, or when they withered, presumably they were unimportant. The Ego, depending on the reactions and responses of other people, was equally expendable. The Super-Ego, the last demand of the *atman*, was the great disciplinarian of the passions. But what use was he when you slept, or even died? Clearly the objective of the *real* soul was to find the point of detachment from which nothing matters at all: goodness nor badness, morality or otherwise, high aims or wretched deeds, religion, love, philosophy, all of equal unimportance. The attractions of such a withdrawal are obviously enormous: here is the dawn-glory of nihilism. Nobody else ever asked for *that*.

Then I think of the determinations and patience and achievements of Gandhi, the desperation and despair of Nehru; I see my wife with her untiring work and her gentle tender eyes: how will one ever understand?

Somehow or other one has got to try. In the year to come I was to have plenty of time.

7

AT THE Bangalore Club the other day we celebrated the twenty-fifth glorious year of India's Independence and rebirth with a whist drive. It seemed as good a way as any other. In the event, nobody turned up. Far away in Parliament the Prime Minister read some political bromides over the radio. It was all over in half an hour.

'We made a tryst with destiny....' I remember that thin tenor voice through the hot Delhi night, each syllable drifting over an enormous human ocean. 'At the midnight hour, while the world sleeps, India will awake to life and freedom.' Thus Jawaharlal Nehru announcing Independence in 1947. I was young in India then and deeply moved. Now, I suppose, I know the smatterings that pass for understanding and that are the most the stranger shall ever know. If I was allowed to share the Indian nostalgia for the brave days of 1947, I could share the flat disappointment of the empty whist drive and the flagging hopes of today.

India survived as the world's greatest democracy, in so far as the word had any meaning at all. The Government pursued a constitutional policy of equality and social justice, which at the present rate would take about forty million years to achieve. Mrs Gandhi was now the best-selling line in prime ministers ever known, as one was daily obliged to recognise: the cult now transcended anything her revered father ever knew. She was Saviour, Winged Victory and Earth Mother. The cover of the

Illustrated Weekly of India had a pious triptych portrait of her 'inspired by the Hindu concept of the Trimurti, or Trinity of God'. This might have been a bit of a facer for those who understood that what she ruled was at least a secular state.

We lived on slogans. In Delhi the millennium was born once a week with a new chapatti-in-the-sky. A third nuclear station was going up at Kalapaka in Madras, and the official Planning Commission agreed that nearly 300 million people still lived below the barest subsistence minimum – that is, on less than fifty pence a *week*. The Defence budget made enormous claims on revenue, and education was actually moving *backwards* : 70 per cent of Indians were still illiterate, more than in the British days because, of course, there were more of them. The college system was in such a calamitous mess that there were even illiterate *graduates*. After twenty years of central planning the Health Minister admitted that there was no possible means of fixing a date when 600,000 villages would get fresh drinking-water. You could go on quoting these figures unto anaesthesia, which is what almost everyone did.

Of course Mrs Gandhi, as a good socialist and a true patriot, was 'taking steps to abolish poverty' – and proper steps too, on paper : nationalising the banks, abolishing the Princely purses, ceilings on land-owning and so on. They were all reasonable pieces of symbolism; their impact would take centuries so long as the well-to-do could buy themselves out of most dilemmas and the poor could not. Mrs Gandhi says : 'It is important that the common man should feel that Government is reducing the gap between rich and poor.'

Perhaps it seemed all right from Delhi. It just seemed a long way from the 'tryst with destiny', twenty-five years ago.

And yet how glib all these arguments were ! What can

twenty-five years mean in the history of such a place?

And yet.... I was forever repeating the phrase; the whole synthesis of my Indian summer stammered along in the words 'And yet—' As the Old Hand said on my first arrival so long ago, I had read more than was good for me and experienced too little. (The truth was quite the opposite, but I knew what he meant.) I was, for example, continually being reminded of extraordinary things that had in fact happened in my lifetime and of which I had become aware only as incidents of history. For years it never occurred to me that I had personally lived in the same age as the British General Dyer, the mass-murderer of the Punjab. If I thought of him at all it was of some vaguely post-Mutiny figure – a tyrant, to be sure, but in some way disinfected by the years. Yet I had been a schoolboy during the 1919 Gandhi-Congress campaigns, on that April day when the crowd gathered in the Jallianwalla Bagh in Amritsar, the holy city of the Sikhs, when General Dyer took ninety Gurkha and Baluchi mercenary soldiers to that densely crowded square and coldly fired 1,605 rounds into their unarmed bodies, killing 379 and wounding more than a thousand. 'I fired and continued to fire,' said General Dyer at the inquiry. 'It was no longer a question of dispersing the crowd but of producing a sufficient moral effect from a military point of view, not only on those who were present but throughout the Punjab.'

In Britain the sum of £26,000 was subscribed as a testimonial to General Dyer's devoted gallantry. This was the year the peace treaty with Germany was signed at Versailles, and the first two minutes' silence held in memory of the Glorious Dead, among whom were surely not the 379 in Amritsar.

I am eternally surprised that the Indians can ever forgive us. They do so of course because, unlike the Irish, they forget.

I cannot unhook myself from this maddening country; I have been trying too long not to love it. I shall probably leave my ashes here, among the rest, but before I do so I shall doubtless keep on nagging at a society that should have given the world so much, and has given so little.

The Indian bureaucracy, most pervasive on earth, was suddenly not without heart. In Bombay the State Government suddenly suspended the Prohibition laws that for twenty-two years had rendered life in that trying place even more arduous than necessary. Until then only the paleface tourist furnished with a liquor permit could repair to the cheerless Permit Rooms and get his card stamped by the bored and weary police. Abruptly the scene changed, the liberty bell rang, Prohibition was no more. So now would the multitudes of Civil Servants who were employed to enforce the law have to join the breadline? Not so; the Prohibition Minister Mr M. B. Probat announced that while one and all could now drink at will, they could do so *on production of a permit*. The permit would be freely available to anyone 'without any condition whatever'.

The implications of this were very Indian. You could go to a bar if you had your piece of paper. You could get your piece of paper merely by saying that you wanted to go to a bar. *But you had to have your piece of paper.* As it was in the beginning. . . .

*

'You are very cruel to our country.'

'I am sorry.'

And I am truly sorry, because while she is right she is also wrong; I am needlessly and arrogantly harsh, and in a sense impertinently, since from all the futilities and exasperations of India it is the Indians who suffer more than I, or more lastingly. But I am not cruel; India is cruel.

'I am no harder on the country than you are. My impatiences and frustrations are trivial and passing, your regrets are inborn and indelible.'

'I have compassion, you have only criticism.'

It is untrue, but I can never really make that clear. Along come the double standards again. I suppose it is true to say that here – in this incomparable evening garden, on the satin turf over which has been laid a soft and costly carpet, with the silver trays of drinks borne discreetly among the guests, with the amber-lit verandah behind and the rising moon above – here, perhaps, I feel compassion diminish. This India would mock compassion; it has everything it wants. It also has, for the moment, everything I want and feel in the mood perversely to enjoy.

We are spending the evening in the home of the brothers Thangavalu and Ethiraj. They are rich. They are also very kind. They and their wives and children and grandchildren and collaterals of all kinds represent the charm and stability of an Indian family at its best, all its accepted cohesion and loyalty. We have nothing comparable in the West. This gentle secure evening among the generations is tranquillity and assurance – the other side of the coin from the brittle encounters to which we have been so much exposed. The joint family of Thangavalu and Ethiraj has the deep-rooted secret of the best of India. So I say, sitting in the armchair on the soft carpet on the barbered turf, which the moon above and fifteen rupees' worth of imported whisky in my hand, and my wife nearby, blending into this sylvan scene as she blends into every scene.

Somewhere perhaps a mile away other families are prov-

ing the same unity of love and dependence embraced together asleep on the grimy pavement, the only home they
ever had or ever will have, and yet contained within the
invisible walls of their privacy, which cannot be violated
even by pity.

'That is not compassion, that is sickening sentimentality.'

'I am only trying to make an analogy. To show I am
not being critical, as you say, of the comfort of this home
and the generosity of our hosts.'

'I suspect you of being ironic. It is one thing Indians do
not appreciate.'

I suggest we ask Nataraj, one of our innumerable relatives, a worldly man of both means and good humour, who
spends his life on the outer rim of social groups, surveying
them sardonically.

'I was trying to say that there is some quality about
Indian family love that transcends – or *can* transcend, shall
we say – the material factors. I admit I am leaning over
backwards in my argument, but could you call it spirituality?'

Nataraj contemplates his long lime-juice-and-gin.

'How foolish everyone is about this Indian spirituality.
Our fault, of course. We had to have something to brag
about that the West doesn't have. The fact is, of course
– though why should I tell you this? – we are the most
materialistic peoples on earth. In the sense that we adore
money. Worship it, almost literally.'

'——' I begin, but if Nataraj is hard to start, he is
harder to stop.

'In the old days, I dare say, things grew easily enough in
India, and it was warm; people didn't have to work
especially hard and so they didn't. Except for a few who
did, and who grew wealthy pretty simply. When the days
of famines and hardships came they naturally came to be
looked on as fortunate beings: why not. By and by they

156

came to dominate the considerations of the poor masses as being *inherently* great, by virtue of being well off, so the Indians who can synthesise anything made these wretched people symbols of greatness and divine favour and all the rest of the poppycock.

'We Indians can rationalise anything, you must know that by now. Failure we understand, we simply put it down to something going wrong in our past lives, which is hardly our responsibility, or we'll explain it by the schemings and treachery of our friends. Chances are we'll be right there. Indians get great satisfaction out of destroying one another. Intrigue is our mother's milk. We say: "He is an excellent fellow, but...."'

The moon has now risen in unexampled glory behind some huge old tree. The warm air is like a caress, and it now carries a gentle scent of myrtle. I try to light a cigarette. Match after match breaks in my hand, occasionally sending an incandescent speck onto the lawn.

'Really, these damned matches. Twenty-five years of independence and they still can't make a workable matchbox; how *can* it be?'

'I have now been hearing you say that a dozen times a day for months. Why not start a matchbox factory? It's obviously badly needed.'

'It would destroy the economy. Any manufacturer of anything that absolutely and reliably worked would have the Indian industrial community on the ropes. Indians *like* matches that don't work. Or maybe every one in four. It is a match's *dharma* to work or not, as destiny decides.'

'Then if you won't start an efficient matchbox-factory, will you just once stop grousing about the ones we have got? That's what matches are like; doubtless they could be improved, and so could everything, as you keep saying.

If you don't like the matches, quit smoking. How is that for adaptation?'

It is my *dharma* forever to lose arguments.

If this were a film we would now cross-fade to the conversation into which we are now absorbed: the younger sons are being languidly intense about the political past. They are reluctantly curious about me, who can remember what they cannot. The dialogue moves in and out, back and forth, like the boys themselves. I am saying rather doubtfully that if ever I go to Delhi my first obligation is a visit to the Rajghat by the Jumna river, the place where they burned the body of Gandhi. I learned this habit from Vincent Sheean.

'Really, you old romantics. I wonder: do you still suppose that nothing became the old British Raj like its abdication?'

'I suppose I do. You don't?'

'James, dear boy, you created us in your image and you did it well, and that was the end of us. Who canonised M. K. Gandhi? You did, all the moist liberals. Have you been to Bengal lately? Have you talked to the students – or the chaps who would be students if there were anywhere open left for them to study? I assure you Gandhi's a forgotten man now.'

'Not by me.'

'Not by you. Okay, did you ever go to jail in the old days?'

'Did you?'

'No, silly. I tried. They sent me back to school.'

'Tough luck.'

'It could still happen. When that madame in Delhi has got all out of us that she wants. Are we not your famous submissive Hindus? Do you resent it if I say we crave a leader – any leader?'

'You're talking like a child.'

'Allow me to say you're talking like a sentimental moralist. You dislike human physical suffering, hunger, blood and so on, because instinctively you think it's yours. You're a walking conditioned reflex. The world is made of suffering and hurt. You should know; you Europeans have your wars every twenty years. Not us Indians. We are the cult of the immobile. We don't contend, we absorb. We absorb everything. We took the Buddha, we invented him, we revered him, then when he became argumentative we sanctified him and made him our tenth incarnation. That settled him. We accepted him, we digested him, we excreted him. We have nearly done that to you.'

'More easily, I should think.'

Smiling, the boy offers me a match. It strikes first time.

Moni says: 'Why do you do it, love? They mean no harm. They sound like fascist brutes....'

'No they don't, that's just it. They're sweet and kind and generous. And so long as they run their kind of society in their kind of way it's doomed, don't you think?'

'Dear man, they've inherited generations of this. It isn't malice, it's biology.'

'What about the Minister there – your own Minister? You said only yesterday....'

'I know about the Minister. I know how the Minister lives, and I know the way his household is run on public funds, and how he's basically dishonest, or you would say so. He was at school with Thangavalu. But at least Thangavalu doesn't....'

'Thangavalu doesn't run for office.'

'Do you suppose that if he did he couldn't buy three times the votes the Minister buys?'

*

159

'Now you know what it is to be a minority,' says Moni.

'My dear, I've always known. I'm a kind of permanent international minority. Once upon a time we brandished it, now we apologise for it. Nothing to do with race, it's to do with character. My sort of minority is because I haven't got the confidence of a ruler and I haven't got the background for a citizen. I can't even speak proper Tamil. I'm useless here and yet I'm happy here.'

'With matches that don't work and corruption and indolence and submission and superstition and funny bathrooms.'

'I know.'

'Because here you're indulged and spoiled and liked, and when that happens you can be happy here, and when there's something nasty in the woodshed you can wallow in censure.'

'At this point,' I say, looking at the mad moon above, 'in every Indian film, they burst into song, and gaze into the twin pools of treacle....'

'Those obese middle-aged juvenile leads!'

'Those glossy Madrasi heroines!'

We strike an absurd theatrical attitude. Everyone pretends not to notice.

*

We had come to Madras, which we both love, although it is hard to say why. This birthplace of the seventeenth- and eighteenth-century commercial Raj is now spoken of by non-Southern Indians rather as the English speak of Wigan. My grandfather's copy of the ninth edition of the *Encyclopedia Britannica* of 1883, which is still the best of all editions and which I continually consult for pleasure rather than for information, is quite scornful about Madras. It produces 'few manufactures, and those of inferior quality', the town 'presents a disappointing appearance, possessing not a single handsome street'. The inhabitants are 'laborious, frugal, pleasure-loving, omnivorous in diet, quite educated, and very fanatical.... The Madras roadstead is liable to be swept by hurricanes of irresistible fury.'

In spite of all this I have a sort of trust in Madras. I like its dimensions, the lowness of its buildings, the half-hearted nature of its enterprise, its steamy heat, its good-natured acceptance of its provincialism. Madras has not the second-hand self-importance of New Delhi nor the hysterical ugliness of Bombay, it is a million miles from the despairing horrors of Calcutta. It is an agreeable, rather boring place; it is the sort of place I would be if I were a town.

8

In the south of India, where live what my wife calls her aboriginals, it becomes easier to understand how offensive to a cultivated Indian an object like the Taj Mahal, for example, can be. The Taj Mahal is a famously graceful piece of architectural rhetoric, its minars and domes symbolise 'India' to the West almost more than any other single object; its likeness is on every printing of Indian travel promotion. It took twenty-two years to build and cost several fortunes; every guide will give you a different figure. Indeed it has style. Nevertheless it is a monument erected by an occupation force, a foreign gesture in a foreign taste. The Taj Mahal is more than the despot Shaj Jehan's monument to a wife who died after bearing fifteen children in fifteen years; it is a building that says firmly: 'The Moghuls were here.' It is the arrogant expression of conquerors who believed (as did Sir Osbert Sitwell in the 1940s) that Hindu art and architecture was repulsive, greasy and vulgar, and who set about destroying every major Hindu temple they could get their hands on. They were vandals, albeit they built the Taj Mahal – and for all that the various Moghul versions of Delhi must have been a more pleasing sight than that of the late King George V. The grandeur of their buildings is oppressive and arrogant, the expression of the Islamic *ubermenschen*. The beauty of the Taj Mahal makes some Indians want to be sick.

However, when the British took over India it was the conquering Muslim rulers they treated with and not the Indians. They learned about India from the Nawabs and the Nabobs. The language they learned was a variant of Persian, not Sanskrit, let alone Tamil or Telugu. It was one more aspect of a theory I have long developed: the peculiar affinity of the English ruling class with Islam. It expressed itself in generations of British favour to Muslims in India at the expense of Hindus; in the Middle East in tacit preference for Arabs against Jews, and for much the same reasons: Hindus, like Hebrews, tended to be clever and even literate, and certainly argumentative, while Muslims shared many of the deep-seated characteristics of the Anglo-Saxon élite – an intuitive resentment of culture, an amicable contempt for women, a proclivity for riding about on horses, a pleasure in discipline, a covert homophilia. However that may be, it was the Moghulistic or Mohammedan aspect of India that became implanted in the English mind from the days of John Company down, with an occasional shove of impetus from writers like Kipling, which is why to this day the Taj Mahal is to tourist India what the Pyramids are to Egypt, only rather more dishonestly.

One of the Indians' problems in this regard is of course the fact that Islamic art, being aseptic and austere, is far more generally acceptable than classic Hindu art, which is voluptuous and sensual and at its best most explicitly sexual. It celebrates copulation and its variants in the most affectionate and fanciful way. Islamic custom denies the plastic artist the right to represent the human form; the old Hindus were obsessed with it and dealt with little else. Representations of the Taj Mahal travel the world on picture-postcards; accurate photographs of the carvings of Khajaraho would be seized by the Customs.

The twenty-two temples at Khajaraho in North India,

which are inspected as masterpieces of sculpture in the Nagara style by a very few elderly students, and for different reasons by countless more amateurs, are probably the most concentrated agglomerations of erotica in the world. They are, as a friend of mine once observed, no more nor less than an enormous stone fucking textbook, a manual of sexual acrobatics. They were created almost a thousand years ago. In a country that today formally bans the most chaste and tentative kiss on the cinema screen, and where teenagers of opposite sexes rarely hold hands in public, Khajaraho serves to show how times have changed.

In the days after Independence, when the new puritanism swept India as for a while it sweeps all revolutionary societies, the New Men were at a loss to know what to do about the statuary of Khajaraho. There were some who were for blocking the whole thing off, in the interests of public morality (for all that Khajaraho had been there since the days of King Canute) but when consideration was given to the value of the tourist dollar better counsels prevailed. It may yet be some time before that Taj Mahal is replaced on the Air India posters by the lovely phallic convolutions of Khajaraho.

There was, as I say, nothing greatly distinguished about Madras. It had a vast beach along the Bay of Bengal, one of the longest and least corrupted left in the world. We thought we might make a small house there, where the sands came up over the seagrass to a small fishing village, some miles out of town. I have always loved fishing villages. We went so far as seriously to investigate an available acre which we could just possibly have afforded, there in a place off the coast road to Mahabalipur where everyone said the heat would roast us and the salty winds would first corrode us and then blow us away. For a while we yearned for it. I often remonstrated with myself for these loose romanticisms. I made drawings for the simplest kind of habitable house. We even saw an architect; if we realised every last penny of assets genuine and speculative we could have just done it, and started from nothing.

It was a pleasant flight of fancy.

How could I ever make a living on a beach in Tamil Nadu? No doubt we could live cheaply enough. We rarely eat meat, and fish and vegetables should have been cheap enough, but however exiguous an income was needed it had to be *something*, and I could see nothing there for me. I might as well set up business at the foot of Mount Everest – better, in fact, the world treads a path to the Himalaya that it does not do to Madras.

I suppose it was part of this *enracinement* process that was obsessing me; my new-found emotional security seemed to demand some kind of symbolic territorial stability to justify it, and I was now emotionally stimulated to the point of drama: I wanted to live on an Indian beach. My wife compounded my fantasies.

'We could build the house on stilts to escape the sand-drifts.'

'A long verandah with a heavy tiled roof; you see those tiles in the village.'

'No heating problems. Oil lamps are cheap. Should you need a telephone?'

'Why a telephone when I have no trade?'

My wife's changes of mood are electrically swift.

'What do you know about Indian villages?'

'Little enough. Except a bit.'

*

More than in any other country in the world India *is* the

village. Everybody spouts this truism; nobody really comprehends it. The 600,000 villages are where *eighty per cent* of all Indians live. This is a remarkable consideration. Flying over India one looks down at what one knows (for one has been endlessly told) is a country overpopulated to the point of suffocation – and for three-quarters of the time one sees nothing, nothing except an immense ochre-coloured emptiness, as barren of life as the rind of the moon. But only travel on the surface of this vast place and you begin to understand: nowhere is *wholly* deserted; somewhere in every frame of vision is someone: a solitary man behind a plough, a boy with a buffalo awash in a pond, a frieze of women waiting at a well; no scene is wholly lifeless, ever.

Yet an Indian village has not grown as villages grow in Europe or America, or even in China, with a recognisable nucleus or core, accreting about a church or a hall or even a store; however small the Indian village it is not cohesive but divisive. For generations it has conformed to the Hindu necessities of social separation and the avoidance of ritual pollution; even now, and presumably forever, it will symbolise the hierarchical factor even of poverty, with the upper-caste farmers grouped with their well and shrine, the middlemen and craftsmen clustered to themselves, the non-caste shoemakers and cleaners still separated again: an immutable pattern.

A village is also ageless, without history or chronology. The mud walls grow out of the soil and soon crumble and return to it; nothing is new, nothing is old. Everything is of now, or of an immeasurable past.

In the days of my brash and impertinent inexperience I once went to a village in the South.

At that time when I was learning – and it is just as true today – if you took a circle about three hundred miles in diameter including the contiguous corners of Madras and the States of Hyderabad and Mysore, you had a place known in terse officialiese as a Scarcity Area. This was where the monsoon failed. The rain that should have fallen did not fall, no one knew exactly why, nor ever will. Without rain the crops failed, when the crops failed people starved, and that was that. I had seen a great deal of hunger and indeed starvation in post-war Europe; that could be explained by human aberrations, or criminalities, like wars and nationalist fatuities of one kind or another; hunger is different from famine. Here people were obliged to die simply by the perversity of their environment, by the simple fact that nature had betrayed them. This was something I knew nothing about then, just as nobody knows anything about it now, however sincerely and angrily they protest from afar. A hundred thousand lives, more or less, do not drag at the emotions when read about in long-range newspapers, the more so if they are Asian lives, which are brief and uncountable and expendable anyway. Famine, for full bellies, is the biggest bore in the world.

Thus I had my first experience of the countryside. The word somehow suggests something altogether different from those endless horizons, those arid plains studded with sudden outcrops of sculptured rock, the glaring skies. Miles from railways, even from roads, were clusters of established life with intricate names like Hanumantharayanagudi and Devaresgondanadoddi. For no reason at all, or so it seemed, a wilderness of stony plain would be punctuated by a collection of huts built of mud and roofed with palm thatch, windowless, doors guarded by the Hindu thread of mango-leaves, dark and secret boxes shared by family and cattle. To such a place I came in an old car, with a haversack of sandwiches and soda-water bottles. It was a strangely rash and ignorant and cruel thing to do, had I only known.

I arrived on ration-day, among the Foodgrains. For a long time I had supposed this to be a pedantic word for rice. Here it was *ragi*, and *jola*, and *haraka*, and *navano*, and *save*, and *saje*; seeds which in Europe one would never see except perhaps at the bottom of a birdcage. Mostly it was *ragi* – we call it, I believe, black millet. Of this each person got twelve ounces a day, never more, occasionally less. On this they had to work. At full pressure it took three Indian peasants to do in an hour what one English farmhand could have done in fifteen minutes.

I walked a mile or two up the track past the brilliant flame-trees and laburnum; somehow the place was profligate with useless beauty. Then I came back to the hut that served as meeting-place for the *panchayat*, the ration-store, the general rendezvous, and they gave me some papaya and a *pan*, as I was a guest. I sat alone on the floor while the village gathered around, observing critically yet indulgently, peering in the door, dark shaven heads coloured with esoteric marks in lime and yellow earth. Outside the solemn grey water-buffalo dreamed at their tethers, the families of monkeys disputed overhead. A million insects moaned around on their trivial occasions and the air was alive with gaudy birds. It was strange and bitter that this land could support so much teeming life – almost everything, it seemed, except man.

So the peasant, dimly conscious of the fact that someone or other was running his country, but resting sure that whatever happened it would not be him, went on his way less concerned with the fact that he would starve tomorrow than that he was hungry today, cursed with his irremovable load of debt, victim of the old philosophy, compounded equally of Brahminism and Anglo-Saxon, that it is dangerous to let the poor learn to think.

In a couple of days I was picked up from the village by the old car and drove away to their courteous farewells.

By staying in the hut that had been the store for their tiny stock of grain I had of course polluted it; where they had had a few pounds of edible *ragi* they now had none.

In newer times I had a friend around there. At moments of special disaffection and regret I would go to Hyderabad to see my friend, who is a very great Indian indeed, although I do not suppose many people knew his name. I met him some twenty-five years ago in the Punjab when India was seething and contending on vast levels of political destiny, but my friend was teaching people how to bore tubewells and run basic co-operatives. It was a brief enough encounter, yet over all those long years we had corresponded with affection; as our families grew up thousands of miles apart we kept in touch. Every time I went to India I would go to visit him for reassurance.

Almost a generation passed, and he moved to the South; his contemporaries all around levered themselves into the big time and the big money, and my friend was still out in the countryside administering his tubewells and his Community Development. He loved the small creations and the service of life, and if India becomes a nation of dignity and honour it will not be through the professional circus and the clockwork orators, but because of my friend and the thousands like him, who would make nothing out of it but headaches and blisters, and perhaps a good night's rest.

Just as we came to India this time my friend's father died far away and he had to make the long journey north for certain duties obligatory to a Hindu son, so I missed our meeting – which goodness knows was always simple enough. Only in India have I come to understand this strangely indescribable business of *dharshan* – the refreshment of momentarily sharing the presence of someone important; it is nothing to do with words. It is strange what a difference it made to me, missing my friend.*

*

Yet even then, serene as I was, secure and confident in the light of day, the bad times would come at night, in the darkness that was more than opaque, that was limitless in space and time, that had no point of reference, that held me fearful of any unguarded movement that might precipitate me into something for which I was not ready, not prepared, since in those moments I could not determine exactly where I was, nor even whom I was. It is a situation I have perhaps tried too often to define, and even exaggerate; maybe it derives from too much sudden and impulsive travel: the dawn dilemma of panic wondering what the inevitable and pitiless day will bring, and above all where. There have been too many places, too many beds, too many anonymous shuttered rooms, too many dripping taps, too many collapses into sleep with too many things undone. I am not afraid of the dark, I am afraid of the night, and I am afraid of the night only because it does not complete the finished day but announces the new one, which would almost certainly be as inadequate as the one before.

Even in India I used – though only occasionally, I admit, the circumstances being so unusual – to wonder how on earth my days were spent, to look back on the curious system that had for so long and for no particular reason permitted me to travel the world almost, though not quite,

---

[1] As this book was being written who should turn up from the blue at our home in London but my friend, miraculously and wonderfully translated to a United Nations post in Trinidad. All those years paid off at last and truly is devotion rewarded: my friend is now the UN adviser for Rural Development to the Caribbean. 'I came to London,' he said gently, 'because I thought you'd like to know.'

as I had wished, to have been party to so much history, and all for the price of doing what in any case I longed to do, describing it. My trade, I had to admit, had done well by me; had I, I wondered, done well by it?

Of all the absurdities in a fantasy-life I think I am fondest of the character who crops up in one of the late Alexander Woolcott's essays in literary fretwork, and who in anticipation of a sojourn in Germany had set himself to learn its language, word by word. For some reason the enterprise was called off, and in exasperation he diligently began to unlearn his German day by day, and in the same manner. By the time he came into the story he was announcing triumphantly that he had that very morning succeeded in forgetting the word for 'house'.

For my part, I spent much vanished time absorbing the creeds and jargon of my trade, only to find, after years of application, that if they existed at all one was better off without them, and the shedding of knowledge thereafter was so accomplished that now I can barely recall coming to terms with it at all. When I am asked how, or even why, I entered journalism (and I cannot say it now happens as often as I could wish) I ramble and equivocate. Does anyone ever 'enter journalism' as a conscious act of decision? Do we not all drift and sidle in, awkwardly or inadvertently, hoping to become MPs or Queen's Counsels or property millionaires or Graham Greenes, yet finding in Grub Street first a *pis aller* and finally a trap? Some people must indeed do the thing in cold blood, or the Schools of Journalism could hardly stay in business, not to speak of the earnest thoroughbred Faculties in American universities. I met a man once in Bangkok who deeply daunted me by saying that he had Majored In Current Affairs. How do you do that? It is my belief that mostly, god knows, we are tramps. We know a man, we scratch a piece, we get a job – and, lo, we have Entered Journalism.

For me the process was oblique enough, since for some years I was under the unaccountable delusion that I was born to be a draughtsman, or, as we said then, an artist, and I worked hard on this fruitless activity. The culmination was a day of especial insolvency in Paris when I sold a remarkably bad drawing to *Figaro* for which I was somehow paid twenty-five francs. This was exactly the sum for which twenty years later you could buy the whole paper. My understanding of economics is such that for years I could not rid myself of the impression, against all the evidence, that things were getting cheaper.

All this happened in another life, and is of no matter now; I must have concluded in my teens that on the whole writers could get away with more than artists. In retrospect I am far from sure I made the right choice; however, the years allow me a personal reaction to the recondite and complex subject of the Freedom of the Press. I will say that I have availed myself of it in pretty fair measure; now as a client of the institution I regard it with equal jealousy. The freedom of the Press is a thing I hold in concern, as I do the freedom of the greengrocery business, or that of the Boilermakers' Union, or the french-polishing trade, or the Miners, or the White Slave Traffic, or indeed every freedom except that of venal or ignorant politicians to corrupt the affairs of decent men with impudent or dangerous legislation. The freedom of the Press in its commercial sense is of equal importance to any of those. Does one talk of the freedom of the Press, or the freedom of the pressman? A newspaper's liberty is notoriously modified and inhibited by a multitude of factors: libel laws, D-Notices, cost of newsprint, restrictive trade-union practices, vicious governmental edicts, the cupidity of proprietors, the Official Secrets Act, drunk and capricious reporters, embittered and neurotic sub-editors, idle and opinionative freelances, the flat-racing season, many assorted myths concerning royalty, the behaviour of other papers. One could moralise about this till the cows came home.

These reflections seemed inane indeed, there in Madras, daily returning to our beach, talking about prevailing winds.... And then, a thousand miles to the north, the fighting began.

It is a morbid thing to contemplate lukewarm history. The catastrophe in Bengal is not long enough ago in years for its meaning to be truly evaluated; long enough in months for its impact to be blunted. In any case I was not, strangely, really involved with the agonies of the rape of East Bengal that finally brought forth the painfully deprived infant Bangladesh. So many people better informed than I have defined that singularly obtuse cruelty. I can now recall the dreadful dilemma that came upon Bengal that summer only in so far as very soon it was to become my dilemma too.

It was, for once, none of my business. Nobody asked me to go to Bengal. I was part of no paper, no publication. It happened during my Indian summer; the gong rang, and I, in my role of Pavlov's dog, responded. Nothing I ever did was so impulsive and needless.

When the fighting began in March, in the aching heat before the rains, nobody outside the subcontinent paid much attention — another Asian calamity; was there not always an Asian calamity? Had there not been a killing typhoon in Bengal not long before, and was this not also Bengal, now dying for some other reason? Some places are committed to catastrophe — of nature, of politics, wars or tidal waves, and in the end it came down to the old cry: help. And nobody knew how to help, nor knows yet.

There is no point in going into the polemical arguments of how this tragic mess came about. The irony then was that this brutal denial of humanity arose from Pakistan's first tentative experiment in democracy. After thirteen years of military rule a civil election was at last held — but the people of East Pakistan, separated from the dominant west wing of the nation by a thousand miles of Indian territory and an unbridgeable gulf in human character, voted in what President Yahya Khan considered to be the wrong way: they asked for a measure of autonomy. The Bengalis are a very peculiar people — in the real sense of peculiar: they are different, exceptional, with different traditions, a different language, a different culture, an absolutely different sense of identity from the Pakistanis of the other ruling half, who had exploited them mercilessly. They expressed this by electing Mujibut Rahman's opposition Awami League by a vast majority. So President Yahya Khan sent in the army to correct this democratic aberration, with the bloody results we were only now beginning to hear about, down in the south.

It was strange, after all those years, to be on the edge of what by any standards was, or should have been, a happening of spectacular importance — doing nothing, writing nothing, going nowhere, keeping my mouth, albeit reluctantly, shut about the whole affair. The clink of Pavlov's bell was already very faintly sounding from the north.

The wretched melodrama of East Pakistan, the pitifully squalid tale of Bangladesh, with its crudities played out in the dark, confused by lies and compassion and ignorance, manipulated by self-seekers in safety — what an indictment of soldiers' rule, of international cowardice, of bureaucratic bumbledom, of neighbourly opportunism, above all of the irresponsible pretensions of my own trade.

It may well be a long time before the Indian press lives down its record over the Bangladesh story. From the start it came as a gift for the more hysterically cheapjack chauvinists, just as the drama of death found an echo in the heart of honest Indians. Between these factors, all newspaper professionalism fell to bits. For an old reporter it was something to make the heart cringe. Everything soared into dreamland. Hardly any Indian correspondents actually went to the scene to see what was happening, and those who did approach as near as they could were through no fault of their own wholly inexperienced at that kind of work, derivative and immature, filing away their half-baked Hemingway in an orgy of wish-fulfilment because, one sadly supposed, this was the Indian line. I was deeply depressed, and even more so was the core of serious and concerned Indian journalists who had so long been my friends, and who viewed this jejune amateurism with a helpless regret.

When I once protested I was assailed by a columnist in an Indian paper, who wrote that 'as a former Beaverbrook wage-slave I was well qualified to spot chicanery's cloven hoof'. It did not matter; he courteously and publicly apologised later, but he could have done his homework.

My own regrets were expressed by a very small part of the Indian press itself. The *Hindustan Times Weekly* on 2 May 1971 editorialised:

Credibility is vital. It is this that has been damaged by the unfortunate lack of professionalism displayed by the Indian print and sound media in their coverage of the fighting in Bangladesh. Objectivity has too often been overwhelmed by emotion. The terrible killing of unarmed men and women, young and old, by the Pakistan Army has been well documented by independent sources ... the solidarity of the people in defence of their democratic rights and liberties found spontaneous echo in Indian minds and hearts. The extravagance in reporting these events in the Indian Press stemmed from a num-

ber of factors : lack of military experience among news-
men, unfamiliarity with military terminology which was
loosely used or even misunderstood; a gullibility that
resulted in uncritical acceptance of unauthenticated reports in an unconscious mood of wish-fulfilment ... and,
unforgivably, the element of competition....

The impression was created that heavy fighting was
waging everywhere, that cities were rapidly changing
hands, that frightful casualties had been inflicted on the
Pakistan Army, that a Bangladesh military victory was
imminent. This was an exaggerated picture. The sub-
sequent contradictions and confusions and the credibility gap this has created reflects poorly on the Indian
press, and in the long run will be seen to have done
more damage to the cause of Bangladesh, as well as to
this country, than is generally realised.

We fretted awhile in the emollient air of Madras, so
far away from trouble. Our bit of beach began to fade away
in the troubles of Bengal.

The headlines as usual reflected no reality, only words.
It seemed clear even through the hyperbole of the press
that Bengal – poor, tense, hysterical, forever on the edge
of some disaster or another – could not possibly handle
this refugee situation unaided. The clamant headlines
shouted at Mrs Gandhi's government with all kinds of
pressures – from well-wishers, ill-wishers, patriots, oppor-
tunists, sentimentalists and conspirators – to solve the problem in the obviously simple and explosive way, of going
to war. Yet (one thought at the time) India was not ready
for war nor ever would be ready for war; India was a
producer of politicians, tax-collectors, speechmakers, of
foreign articles manufactured under licence and soldiers
moulded to a foreign pattern, regulations printed in another image long ago. The Chinese invasion of 1962 and

176

its peculiar humiliations to the famous Fourth Division had surely proved all that; had not the Chinese, with Bengal at their mercy, turned round and gone home simply because no invader in his senses could possibly *want* Bengal?

In these considerations, as in so many others, I was of course wrong; President Yahya Khan's Pakistan was a stupider and more blundering adversary than Chairman Mao's China, and this I should have known.

In Madras there was no way of learning the truth of what was going on. I had, I suppose, no greater reason to know it than anyone else, except that years of conditioning had made me restless when sad and important events were taking place beyond my horizon, and I had perhaps fairly good professional reasons for doubting the printed nonsense with which we were daily drenched. There was no purpose whatever in my pursuing the matter further except the basest of motives: curiosity. However, Moni's time to return home to England had come; I had a little time left to spare. We said goodbye at the airport of Madras: she leaving for London, I for Calcutta.

9

EXPERIENCED TRAVELLERS argue and contend over their images of what is best remembered, of beauty or pleasure or tranquillity or fun, but among them is rarely any difference of opinion about what is worst, the most irredeemably horrible, vile, and despairing city in the world; few who know it will dispute that this place is Calcutta. The urban awfulness of Calcutta has become a cliché of such dimensions that one flinches from even trying to say more about it, with such lasting and eloquent disgust has every aspect of this appalling place been described since Kipling called it 'the city of dreadful night'.

The inhuman cruelty of Calcutta defies the normal language of odium; its total wrongness has become base-measure of injustice, and its paradoxes are a platitude. It is immensely rich, and its poverty is of such an inescapable, all-pervadingly intrusive kind that generations of sociologists, reformers, planners, do-gooders and destroyers have, in the end, thrown up their hands and hopelessly retreated, loudly proclaiming that Calcutta's wretchedness has gone not only past redemption but beyond description. This, I should say, is probably true. Its physical ugliness is surpassing; at no time can Calcutta have had any aspect of a man-made town other than the crude and pinchbeck, or of a monumental Victorian durability that never mellows with age but grows unkempt and smelly with senility. Everything in Calcutta transcends the ordinary extremes.

Its excuse for existence is the greatest of negatives: that anyone who has lived in Calcutta can never again find serious fault with anywhere else. It is the nadir of all those base values of British Imperialism that were perpetuated by India herself: that is to say, the proclaimed indifference to human life. In Calcutta, most people are debris, and only too clearly know they will never be anything else.

This place could have been designed as the demonstrable end-product of civic disorganisation. I have often wondered how more explicitly the twentieth century could have produced its symbol of inequality. India is a country of beggars; nowhere but in Calcutta is there beggary of such a ubiquitous, various, ever-present and inescapable kind. From the moment you walk into the public ways until the moment you lock your bedroom door the beggars are with you, around you, almost inside you; they are like flies in the Sinai desert, seemingly part of the atmosphere. After so many arrivals and departures in Calcutta I can sometimes feel part of an endlessly changing yet forever static Breughel scene: I recognise even the individuals, or their reproductions – the mutilated cripples, the grotesques, the limbless things grovelling along on blocks strapped to their stumps, the apparently immortal mobile cadaver whose enormous arms drag his shrivelled trunk along the gutter, the gambolling children who thirty times an hour can burst on cue into the most poignant histrionic tears, the lepers and tertiary syphilitics and pinheads and epileptics and normally starving men and women. Exactly the same cast of characters seems to have been there for twenty-five years.

To a European, and especially to a stranger exposed to it for the first time, this mass industry of organised misery must be a seriously disturbing experience, nothing in his ordinary Western responses equips him to come to terms with it: at first conscience rides on his back wherever he goes, as indeed it well might; the loose *paise* in his pocket would feed one of these abject ruins for several days. But of course it will not be enough for the crowds of competitors, alert for inexperienced compassion, who rush in moaning for equity. On the second day he sees a starving mother to whom he has given his coppers carefully counting them, and pursuing him with imprecations for more. He will come to fear the beggars, embarrassment turns into resentment, and soon into a sort of hatred: the destroyed and dreadful people of the streets are no longer victims of the cruelty of Calcutta but its creatures, themselves both exploited and exploiters. The first time the stranger brushes off a beggar with an oath he has both won and lost. He is judging India by the standards of Europe, or of America. He does not realise that the Indian beggar is concomitant to the piety even of the poor; the act of charity is the important thing, however trifling and to whatever charlatan it may be.

There was such a man at the end of Chowringhee; every day he had been there and interrupted me; not only every day but four, five times a day he had interposed himself between me and the kerb I had to cross. It was a changeless gesture, wholly predictable – he limped, he crouched, he moaned absently and reached out with his handless stumps. Then he stood four square directly in my path, refusing to move; it was always I who had to change my course and swerve aside, so that he could reproach me with his empty wrists for having avoided him, compounding my guilt.

Then I did a terrible thing: when for the fiftieth time he shambled to his appointed place immediately before me I did not step aside but continued on my way, walked into him, *through* him; I could not have done it had he not goaded me to cruelty. It was like walking into a paper bag full of twigs. There was nothing to him but shards

180

and sinews, and he reeled away from my slight impact and disintegrated like an abandoned marionette. It was as though I had attacked and destroyed a doll. I did nothing but continue on my rightful way, but I was now manifestly an aggressor, a tyrant, a Hun, a colonialist; I could never testify to his calculated provocation. The next moment he had scuttled away like an insect; there was now for me no penance.

That afternoon he was there as usual; he shambled forth and stood before me exactly as before, not the slightest variation in his stance or role. I walked around him, as in the past, as I always shall.

*

Indians will debate for hours about their own nature, their neighbour's nature, the ethnic differences which distinguish one from another and come to no conclusion, but everyone finds it simple to define the Bengalis. They are quick, they are clever, they are brilliant, they are mad, they are cultivated, they are hysterical, they are artists, they are revolutionaries, they are poets, they are murderers, they are victims; above all they are Bengalis, neither Indians first nor Hindus nor Muslims first; they are a special people. Non-Bengalis believe this, and Bengalis believe it too. All the Roys, Banerjees, Sens, Sarkars, Dutts, Basus, Boses: folklore would have it that they are all geniuses or paranoiacs. In Bengal a train-driver can be lynched for arriving twenty minutes late (and has been). Yet Bengal produced Jyoti Basu, the most impressive Communist in India. It also produced Rabindranath Tagore, Bankim Chatterji, and Satyajit Ray.

I once called upon Satyajit Ray in my role of *chela*, or disciple; I followed the grubby narrow street in which he lived and up to the small second-storey apartment he inhabited: no other film celebrity had ever lived with less ostentation than the man who had made *Pather Panchali* and *Aparajito*. He was a wonderful man, tall and with a huge face; he wore a kurta and pajama and sat in a little room among a wilderness of papers and musical instruments, and somehow he loves Calcutta.

'All my life I lived here. Anything that happens in the arts in India happens here. The Bengali writers are writing; the Bengali theatre is full of life. If you want to know how political it is go and work with Utpal Dutt.' (I did: Utpal Dutt is a most celebrated actor-manager whom to call left-wing would be an insulting understatement; for days I followed him with a street-theatre company which could probably never have existed in a less terrible place than Calcutta.)

'Calcutta is the most intellectually exciting place in Asia,' said Satyajit Ray. 'I wish I could divert some of the intellectual emphasis into films, but most of it stays in the coffee-houses. I am afraid this I can understand.'

Nevertheless I know that I shall never love Calcutta. I had arrived by air, which is a preconditioning to trouble.

From Dum Dum airport into Calcutta there was no other transport than the bus; the taxis had decided that for the time being the journey was too dangerous. The day before a group of small gangsters had boarded one of the groaning, smoking, overcrowded buses on the Dum Dum road; a few minutes later there were two shots, and a twenty-five-year-old policeman, pouring blood, was kicked from the bus to die by the noisome ditch at the roadside. He was the sixty-seventh policeman to be murdered in Calcutta that year. Rather more than a dozen people had been murdered in the city during that weekend. The situation was, in its way, normal. Until recently the Calcutta papers carried a daily column: 'Last Night's Murders'; it became repetitious and they gave it up. The

182

airport bus took us into town escorted by a police truck with four riflemen aboard.

It was by any standards the most lowering approach to anywhere. Calcutta is demonstrably the most over-crowded place on earth. It is reckoned to hold about 110,000 people per square mile, which is horrific even for Asia. New York has some 27,000 per square mile; Delhi has 42,000. Figures like that are usually meaningless, but in Calcutta the congestion and density is *palpable*, in the pullulating streets and festering alleys, in the rickety bustees, the Registered Slums — for Indian bureaucracy requires that even a slum must lay formal claim to its ignominy and be registered. For what? Not for reparation, or clearance, only to fulfil the Indian need to record, write down, file away, and forget.

Even the name of the place is rooted in savagery and fear, since Calcutta is called after a cruel image. Among the countless gods and godlings of the Hindu pantheon, symbolising every aspect and aberration of human philosophy, none is more truly unpleasant and fearsome than the wife of Siva the Destroyer, who is sometimes known in Bengal as Durga, but mostly known as Kali the Terrible, who is presented in most of her representations in satanic form, garlanded with skulls and serpents, her tongue dripping blood. On the banks of the Hooghly a temple was built for her, and it is after this repellent goddess that the surrounding township was named: Kalikata.

Down there, now, was the vast Howrah Bridge spanning the Hooghly River like a threat; 87,000 tons of steel in it and you could sense every pound of its weight in that gross and graceless shape. The Howrah Bridge was the father and mother of all traffic bottlenecks, carrying nearly two million and 60,000 vehicles every day, the greatest load of any bridge in the world. They used to say that because of heat expansion the Bridge was four inches longer by day than by night, and I would not dispute it. At the other side lay this great industrial suburb of a million and a half people, without one single town-drain.

It was several years since I had last passed this lump of metallic melodrama, serving my prentice days in the business of films. This was a new calling for me, to which I had come as a kind of calculated challenge to the journalistic trade in which I had spent so much of my life. When the last newspaper on whose staff I had been – the old *News Chronicle*, where I had long been very happy and whose obituary I have written a little too often – was abruptly and untimely crushed, I felt a disenchantment with the whole business and proposed to tie myself to Fleet Street no more. It was very necessary nonetheless to find some means of making a living and, not for the first time, I had to give some serious thought to the future. It seemed improbable that at my time of life I could suddenly make a fortune as a property-developer or a ballet-dancer. What then did I want to do? Only two occupations had ever commended themselves to me: one was writing and the other was communicating, and from my experience they were by no means necessarily the same thing. Therefore – I said to myself in my innocence – I will see if I can write as a sort of personal catalyst and, as for communicating, I would have a go at the medium that appeared to do it most swiftly and to the greatest number, to wit the television, with which I had had until then but a meagre acquaintance. In the earlier days of what was called 'documentary' the system had been that someone went out and shot a film, frequently sponsored by some oil company with money to burn or, worse, a Government department; they edited it into a fine cut, commissioned a music track, and then would say, as an afterthought: What about a *commentary*, by the way? Someone like myself would then be called in to produce brief bursts of words, rigidly tailored to match the frames that someone else had completed long before. It was tedious work, and underpaid at that. Nevertheless it gave me a notion of what it was all about.

I therefore knocked on the door of the BBC with a proposition that in retrospect seems rather less daring than it did at the time. I suggested that what television needed was a visual approximation of a signed personal column, from which if necessary the organisation could dissociate itself, but which could have an intrinsic value not necessarily sterilised by the BBC imprimatur. If a sufficient variety of differing and idiosyncratic views were thus presented, I suggested, a measure of overall balance could be achieved. It seemed to me that to seek a total equilibrium of attitudes, as was the rule, within the scope of, say, an hour was to stultify rather than stimulate; let us therefore annoy and exasperate people in sections, with the assurance that we would equally offend their opponents later. The Corporation did not readily accept this argument, which appeared in some recondite way to run counter to its Charter and to the ghost of the late Lord Reith. After a while, however, it suddenly and unexpectedly agreed to the idea, and set up a series to be known as *One Pair of Eyes*.

However, the BBC organised slots for these opinionative programmes before arrangements could be made for a sufficiency of contending viewpoints, and in the event I found myself doing the first three shows on my own, which was a matter of great satisfaction to me but rather negated the original principle. Still, they were the best and most rewarding programmes I ever did, out of many to come.

We started in India. The films had an essentially autobiographical purpose. Starting in India, however, put me at a disadvantage right away, since there had only recently been made a programme by Malcolm Muggeridge and directed by Kevin Billington on a very similar subject: it was called *Twilight of Empire*, and it took Malcolm Muggeridge through *his* early days in India, and it was of such a matchless excellence that I embarked on my embryo project rather as one would start a play about an incestuous Scandinavian royal family shortly after the opening of *Hamlet*.

As it turned out our respective attitudes were so dissimilar the programmes might have been about different countries.

I had begun by returning to my India of the forties, and in New Delhi I somehow managed to disinter my first official dossier from the mountain of dust-caked files in the Department of Information. This was no small job. The yellowing folder was finally discovered, and there I found my registration: NAME: *Cameron, James*; OCCUPATION: *Journalist*; STATUS: *Temporary Person Passing Through*.

That had been some twenty-five years before, and that is what I must have supposed myself to be.

We called the programme, therefore: *Temporary Person Passing Through*. I imagine we had some minor irony in mind, but it seemed as good a personal definition as any other.

I was directed by a young friend called Dick Fontaine. He had never worked in Asia before, and it was of the greatest importance to him that, whatever befell us in India, there should be no moment of the picturesque, no hint of the accepted and outworn visual beauties that, as he rightly said, had overlain and suffocated every film about India since the medium was invented. It was Dick's plan to make India, if possible, resemble Huddersfield. In principle I wholly agreed; in practice of course the plan began to fall through as soon as the camera turned; it was difficult indeed to film anything in India without some element of the strange and beautiful intruding, even if – and we finally return to the point – we went down beside the horrible Howrah Bridge.

We spent a morning by the *ghats* of the Hooghly River

beside that awful bridge. Nothing could have been more sociologically wretched; every square centimetre of the frame was an image of despair, yet it had a compelling, irresistible beauty. It just is a fact that poverty *is* picturesque, that truly hungry people assume almost balletic compositions, that beggary *is* beautiful. I tried to express this somehow in the film, but of course it sounded as pretentious then as it does now.

Calcutta is obsessive. Having promised not to indulge myself yet again in revulsion and recrimination already I find myself murmuring incantations to protect myself from the pervasions of its degradation and filth and injustice and sadness. But it is a place so adapted to despair that once one has known it one can never again be wholly free. That must be why I had come to Calcutta unasked, at my own compulsion, perhaps because, being so happy, I needed to be hurt.

The last word on the place was written by Geoffrey Moorhouse in his superb book *Calcutta* (1971):

Perhaps there will be another kind of disaster before Calcutta is left to its plague, though this one threatens only the rich in their nightmares. In this haunting horror, the night comes when every poor man in the city rises from his pavement and his squalid bustee and at last dispossesses the rich with crazy ferocity. The arsenals of the rich will be no protection against this onslaught in the close confinements of Calcutta, for there are so many millions of poor here and only a few thousand of rich, and life is very cheaply lived upon a pavement and in a bustee. The poor shadows will come quietly out of their deeper darkness and they will pick off the first few rich in small handfuls, hauling them out of their cars and butchering them on the spot; and when the rich reach for their defences they will be overwhelmed and buried by the numbers of the poor. There will be a signal for this nightmare to become a reality and it will be given by the rickshaw men who have pulled so many rich people round Calcutta like animals all their lives. They will begin to pass it on when darkness falls, as the rich move away to their homes and their pleasures. All over the city and along the Hooghly there will be the sound of bells being tapped one after another against the shafts of motionless rickshaws or upon the sides of lamp posts. As any rich man walks the streets that night he will be followed wherever he goes, from one pool of light to the next, by this dull anvil ring of rickshaw bells. Tap-tap-tap, the signal will pursue him mysteriously down each street; and there will be no shaking it off. It will tell him that his time has come. The time for compassion will be past.

*

My friend Sen was at the Grand to meet me, possessed by demons. The happenings in East Bengal, the murderous outrages of the West Pakistani Army in suppressing the Bengali separatists, peasants, and wholly innocent inhabitants were driving him into transports of anger. He had organised a publicity centre for the refugees on the Maidan across the way from the hotel; out of the millions already streaming into India, he said, thousands had already penetrated Calcutta itself. His refugee-marquee was hung with atrocity-photographs of a lurid and horrible nature.

'People must be told!' he cried. 'People must be made to know!'

'Will it help these poor devils?'

'Of course. Our nation will be enraged and rise in their defence.'

My good friend Sen is a very political Bengali lawyer and an old associate. To draw attention to his many causes he adopted a most extraordinary stratagem: he swam his way to fame. He swam not only the English Channel but, thereafter, every swimmable channel of water in the world – the Dardanelles, the Hellespont, the Straits of Gibraltar, the Palk Strait between India and Ceylon. He even swam through the Panama Canal. He is the most durable swimmer alive. I used once to swim with him in the Habana Libre pool in Castro's Cuba, where there was little else to do; long hours after I had taken to my rum-sour at the poolside bar he would be at his two-hundredth length, like an Indian sealion. Now all that frivolity was long behind him; he was obsessed by the brutal horrors in Dacca and East Bengal.

'You shall go to the frontier and see.'

In the desperate and unpredictable circumstances of the day this required organising; the Pakistan border was now a defence area; very soon to become a battlefield. I had no claim to represent any organisation; I could hardly ask as a sightseer for a place on the conducted bus-tours. However, after all these years government had probably not forgotten me altogether.

I still could not quite understand why I was doing this. I had never before gone anywhere except to write; I had never sought any experience that I had not, in a way, been employed to share. Some sort of reflex response was taking me through the motions now; it was like old times.

Like old times too was the Writers' Building, that sombre relic of old British Bengal that forms an entire side of a big Calcutta square, an immense wilderness of bureaucrats that even for India was striking for its reduction and compression of civil servants into the likeness of battery fowls. It was named for the junior clerks of the East India Company, the 'writers'; it now houses the West Bengal administration. Here the West Bengal secretariat was increasingly desperately trying to sort out the fantastic and accumulating problems of the refugees. Doubtless within this warren might be some sort of authority for me.

Writers' Building represented everything administratively inhuman that the British made and the Indians preserved. It was an immense red-brick pile of an 1880 character wholly unmemorable but for its size. Inside it was more than Dickensian; it was Kafkaesque. Narrow corridors threaded through its many floors, lined with innumerable minute offices – or rather stalls, since they were not dignified by doors, but by swinging chest-high partitions, grey with age and uttering an incessant symphony of tiny squeals from antique hinges. On the stall doors, as it were a racehorse stable, were name boards: 'Deputy Assistant Under-Secretary, Weights & Measures', 'Assistant to the Deputy Secretary, Traffic Dept'. Outside most of them crouched or stood or leaned the ragged line of inquirers or supplicants. Dogs wandered idly about. Dust and waste paper flurried around in little whirlwinds.

Inside each of these cells sat one clerk, with a pen, a set of forms, and rotting piles of ancient files, which clearly no one for many years had dared disturb, the ages had practically cemented them together. Their protruding edges stirred under the fans with a gentle bony crepitation. Everywhere the old fans turned overhead incessantly, quietly creaking, causing a warm breeze to blow the hair and keep the multitudes of forms on the multitude of desks just forever on the point of, but never quite, blowing away.

Somewhere we found a stable door marked: 'Under Secretary, Refugee Rehabilitation'. There, surrounded by what might well have been records of the Indian Mutiny, to which new forms were constantly being added by the chaprassis who passed in procession through the cubicle, vainly trying to seek a number on a useless telephone, watched over the top of his stall door by a crowd of anxious eyes and hearing the faint entreaties from the corridor of those seeking to complicate his confusion, was part of the machine that was already committed somehow to looking after an invasion of East Bengali refugees whose numbers had already passed six million, and continued unabated every hour of the day, and which Mrs Gandhi the Prime Minister had just called 'the biggest and cruellest migration in all history', a definition that was undeniably correct and growing more so every day.

The official, his white shirt clinging with sweat to his ribs, received me with a politeness clearly on the inner edge of neurosis. 'What is your kindly name?' With every goodwill he could not help me about the border; his function was with the refugees already here – in the camps, on the roads, even here in Calcutta itself. There were said, as unreliably as everything else, to be 100,000 in the city already.

'It is an *appalling* problem,' said the poor man unnecessarily, his pen still scratching automatic random marks on his piles of forms. 'If we don't do enough Comrade Basu's Marxists will be after us, and they reckon on thirty per cent of the provincial votes. If we do too much the rest will be after us – they say the expatriates are taking our people's jobs at cut rates. Food prices already up fifty, hundred per cent. We have work-cut-out, as you say. Now they are beginning to talk about cholera....'

And now, in the classic phrase, the rains had come.

The summer monsoon rains in India are not as other rainfall; they droppeth not as the gentle rain from heaven upon the place beneath; they fall abruptly, sensationally, ferociously, torrentially; in the country they can tear away the banks of a watercourse in moments; in Calcutta a normal midtown street can be transformed into a river literally in a matter of minutes. A rain-storm is the only phenomenon that can suddenly and totally bring Calcutta's crazy traffic to a halt; at the height of the deluge the place looks like a dreadful parody of Venice. No system of drains and conduits, least of all the befouled and neglected ones of Calcutta, could cope with this sort of rainfall.

This, less than a hundred miles away, was now falling on the homeless refugees.

So my friend took me off to see the Director of the Border Security Force, the topmost man in that extremely sensitive field. I have never been at my best in the company of high-ranking soldiers or policemen, and the combination of both in one person was a daunting prospect.

I could not have been more surprised if he had turned out to be Noël Coward, or Dr Schweitzer. The Director was a middle-sized, middle-aged gentleman behind a big desk, resembling in no way a master of men or a ranking officer, but rather a bank manager of the kindlier sort, or perhaps a teacher. He took off his glasses with a smile and made us welcome; unlike most such officials the world over he gave the impression of genuine pleasure at being distracted from his work.

Not wanting to waste his time, however, I came respectfully to the point about an official permit for the border regions. There should be no problem, he said, and made a note on a pad. Almost at once the conversation took off in a dozen wholly unexpected directions.

We spoke regretfully of the troubles that were befalling

East Bengal, and inevitably drifted on to the whole subject of Hindu–Muslim relations. Before we knew it, and in some manner that I could never afterwards quite remember, the Director was talking of the influence of the ancient Sanskrit verse on the European Romantic revival.

'It is my impression that Wordsworth never really knew he admired nature until he read translations of Jayadeva.'

Then we were on to the Germans – Schiller, Goethe, even Kant and Hegel. The Director revealed a vast and effortless knowledge of European literature. I was very soon far out of my depth, treading water in a tide of recondite references.

A friend, a man of vigorously practical tastes and boiling political certainties, grew restless. 'While we talk of poets, our brothers are perishing!'

'That is sadly true. Nevertheless....'

My friend grew scathing of culture, and especially that of the Muslims. 'What is the culture of Islam but that of rape and pillage? I can show you photographs from Dacca—'

'That is also unhappily true. But are you summarily going to dismiss the poets Hafiz, Amir Khosrau, for example?'

'Derivative tripe. What's more they're Persian.'

'To be sure,' said the Director soothingly, 'Islam was always new, always divided, nomadic societies ... it was necessary to rely on the stable culture of the Persians.'

The next moment we were debating the substance of the Universe – some analogy had occurred to the Director in the molecular structure of a paperweight on his desk, resembling somehow the solar system. Nils Bohr. Max Planck. Rutherford. Einstein. The Director was well up in physics too. In no time he was illustrating his argument with quotations from Bengali poetry – his own, he had published several small volumes. He was the most improbable policeman I had ever met.

My friend fretted away through this, then suddenly dived into his favourite theory: Human Division, he called it, biology and mind, the physical versus the cerebral. It had been a serious mistake of the Creator to engage the procreative urge and abstract intelligence in the same cortex. However, automation and computers were bringing the total human revolution – work would become a three-day week, a two-day week, a one-day week, a no-day week. By and by there would be no need for actual effort of any kind. We would then dispense with wasteful urges like hunger, survival – above all, sex.

'That might not be altogether an advantage,' said the Director mildly.

'It would be a total advantage!' cried my friend. 'Can you imagine of a more preposterous way of propagating than ours? No self-respecting woman would ever waste time bearing children again. There will be no further need for genitalia, since everything will be genetically engineered....'

'It would certainly knock a hole in Hinduism,' agreed the Director. 'Not much room for the *lingam* and the *yoni*.'

'Right! They will atrophy and wither. There will be no need for limbs. Simple torsos, living in leisure. Maybe not even that. No need for anything, really, except the brain, and that will be made artificially.'

'By what?'

'By itself.'

'So no more bodies, no more eating, no more sex, no more tennis. Just a lot of brains in plastic containers.'

'No, no. I cannot see that there should be more than one – just one!'

'Well,' said the Director, 'it would certainly solve your

political problems. An oligarchy of one unique personality (would it have a personality?) ruling over only itself. Perfect democracy, autocracy, anarchy all in one. And at least', said the Director gently, 'it'll put paid to the poets.'

It was a good cue on which to go out, and we re-entered the earth's atmosphere.

'Everything will be in order tomorrow. It has been a pleasure chatting.'

I believe he really meant it.

10

THE TOWN of Shikapur was roughly on the frontier. I left the car in the Border Security Forces' compound and got a lift to the edge of East and West Bengal, to a township where the Pakistanis were pouring into India like a river through a broken dyke, a beaten, ragged, penniless, plodding line, drained of everything but the compulsion to stay with the herd.

The township normally held some 20,000 people; in the past week about 200,000 more had flooded in. They were still arriving at the rate of about 50,000 a day. They were camped in schools, temples, cowsheds; they had thrown up little matting shelters in stretches of marshland; hundreds of the elderly were merely lying immobile by the roadside where they had found that they could walk no more. The columns never ceased, long unsmiling exhausted lines of gaunt people, their shreds of dhotis and saris in mud-matted rags, heavy bundles of everything on their heads. The rain poured down in a thick pitiless torrent, as it had done for days. All the great Gangelic delta was now a swamp.

A grey-faced official wrung out the tail of his soaking shirt in a futile gesture.

'Strange how we long for this monsoon every year. Bengalis would die without it. And now they're dying because of it.'

Because, I suppose, of the age in which I lived I had been obliged to engage myself in so many situations involving refugees. 'Refugees' – the word itself had almost a generic sound, as it were: Animals, Cripples, Jews, Latvians, Hindus, People. Refugees of one kind or another had been a semi-permanent factor of the world society ever since I could remember. When I was a boy of three we had in our home what were called Belgian Refugees; they were the class of 1914, inconspicuous and individual; as far as I can remember they were those exceptionally out of luck; they were not Social Problems, let alone instruments of massive politics. A generation later came the refugees swarming westwards over Germany; Palestine refugees most ironically dispossessed by those themselves dispossessed; Hindu and Muslim refugees by the hundred thousand crossing each other's paths in the Punjab after Partition; Korean refugees, Vietnam refugees, all presenting their own variant aspects of exile.

I had seen them all, written about them all in various manners of easy professional pity or wholly useless anger; I had never really *done* anything for them except, perhaps, make known a slender part of their sorrow. It is a disturbing thing for a journalist occasionally to consider how far unhappiness and want and martyrdom had become, despite himself, part of his stock in trade; the facts of disaster a kind of raw material for the manufacture of a momentary emotion in people far away, somewhere between the stock market and the sports page.

If that were not so, why was I here at all? Was it possible that I was only responding to some ingrained impulse, like a *voyeur* or a boy who follows fire-engines? I would reproach myself forever if that were true, but it might have been. If so I was to be well repaid.

Of all the mass-migrations I had seen, none had been like this.

These were early days, yet already the influx of refugees was counted in five million? – six million? – nobody knew for sure. How could they? Nobody knew for sure the population even of West Bengal in normal times, whatever *they* were; nobody even knew the population of Calcutta. It is presumably not for nothing that the major unit of Indian counting is the *lakh*, which is 100,000, and the *crore*, which is ten million. In the calculations of Indian calamity, as in the days of princely riches, this would seem to be an inevitable convenience.

All one knew was that in the sudden frantic desolation brought about by the soldiers of President Yahya Khan one certainty emerged: the ten million Hindus who had, in their optimism, decided to stay on in the Muslim state after Partition – committing themselves in their ignorance to twenty-four years of harassment and injustice – had finally realised that their only hope lay in India. (Since in those early days the prospects of an independent Bangladesh were to say the least speculative.) For a time, in the past year, the Hindus of East Bengal had responded to promises of Sheikh Mujibur Rahman and his Awami League, defying the army of Yahya Khan and offering equality to all. That, it seemed, had been another bad bet, for now the Pakistan Government had ordered in the soldiers to crush all these preposterous democratic pretensions with all the military machinery their American armoury could provide. With every little group in flight across the Border came tales of murder, rapine, the burning of crops, destruction of villages. In the nature of such stories many may have been true, many half-true, some apocryphal; the important thing was that everyone believed them to be true, and in consequence the hungry multitudes pouring into India were in a state of high desperation. In any case in the fifty-mile stretch between Krishnanagur and Shikapur one had to believe no more than the evidence of one's senses: the smell of death from the ditches, the sight, beloved of cameramen, of babies suckling at dead breasts and dogs devouring the almost-dead. The even more important thing was that the Indian Government of West Bengal, itself forever on a knife-edge of political crisis, itself the archetype of economic insecurity, was now confronted with this unprecedented and almost unmanageable situation. It could not, as they say, have happened to a more unlucky people.

So I found myself in this township, which I believe, without any certainty, was called Barsat, in the remorseless rain, watching the refugees move in like an incoming tide, filling the rockpools, overflowing them, filling the saturated fields and overflowing them. There was a Reception Centre where, incredibly, they were supposed to register. The queues stood there patiently in the rain, drained of everything. The inoculations were first; without an inoculation card they did not get a ration card. The ration card entitled them to four hundred grammes of rice and two hundred of pulse. Some had been waiting in line already a day and a half for the medical shots; about two were dying every hour. There was a kind of a hospital, already more than a hundred per cent overcrowded. A building behind had already been turned into a cholera ward; it was awash with the faeces and vomit of choleric diarrhoea. Porters with cloths tied across their mouths brought the bodies out and heaved them over a low wall. In this quagmire it was impossible to find a means of Hindu cremation; their week-long struggle to safety would end in the indignity of burial in the sodden ground.

In the months to come there was time to reflect on all this. Pakistan was a nation conceived in fear, born in bitterness, and broken in folly. It took less than twenty-five years to prove to the world, if not to itself, that a nation created out of negatives was founded on sand. In Simla and Delhi back in the forties we had, indeed, been thinking so already.

A nation came into being wholly, and solely, to institutionalise Islam in the subcontinent, in what Mohammed Ali Jinnah argued was a gesture of defence of the Faith against the pre-eminent Hinduism of India. To the creators of Pakistan, nationalism was an instrument and a vehicle of religion; to the leaders of India religion had, and has, no constitutional place in an avowedly secular state. There was a certain amount of humbug in both these attitudes; nevertheless therein lay all the difference in the world between the concepts of the two nations which would otherwise, and certainly should, have grown as one.

Now even in those early days when I was dismally wading through this slough of despond in Bengal, we were already thinking of Pakistan in obituary terms.

The world's reaction to this sorry mess of Bangladesh was initially as confused as the events themselves. The United States, which had provided President Yahya Khan's Army with most of the weapons with which to whip the Bengalis, decided that the débâcle was a matter of Pakistan internal politics. The British swithered and equivocated.

The Chinese perversely came out on Yahya Khan's side, to the consternation of most Bengali Communists who had prematurely jumped on to the Bangladesh bandwaggon as a textbook exemplar of the People's War. India wholly disproved Pakistan's allegations of conspiracy by being herself manifestly caught on the wrong foot by the appalling load suddenly thrust upon her, and even in her deepest difficulties could not shake off her impenetrable and mercenary bureaucracy. A month after I had gone a British voluntary medical team were unable to release their mobile hospital and its vaccines and equipment, flown in by the RAF, because it was held up at the airport by the Customs for days, for want of either an excise payment or an unobtainable official signature.

At the border township I had had enough – of rain, of sorrow, of eating other people's rations, of sleeping in the slime, of debates that ended in despair, of the realisation of total uselessness. I asked if I could find a lift back to Shikapur so that I could go back to Calcutta; even Calcutta offered some sort of improvement on this.

The Indian colonel who had been patient and considerate with me for so long was considerate again; his jeep was ready to leave and there was room for me. We would at least, he said, have a goodbye drink in the Mess. It seemed in the circumstances a callous ambition, but I greatly shared it.

For a few miles our road led us along the refugee trail, against the prevailing stream of the people. The coming of evening seemed in no way to diminish the columns of empty-eyed, stumbling Bengalis, they still trudged into India with their bundles on their heads and their rags in the rain.

'The problem is clearly insoluble,' the Colonel was saying as the bus truck appeared up the road ahead of us, apparently about a half a mile away. It was rolling slightly from side to side, sending up a bow-wave of brown water from its front wheels. From the moment it became visible I knew we were in trouble. Neither the bus nor our jeep was travelling very fast; ordinarily there would have been just room to pass in a chancy safety. But the refugees had narrowed the highway, such as it was, and the surface of the road was now a sequence of pools linked by skid pans of greasy mud. Indian drivers make it a point of honour never to give way until the last moment, and I knew that this could not be many seconds off.

I said : 'We're cutting it fine, Colonel.'

He grunted : 'Take it easy, driver.'

'Thik hai, sahib,' said the driver, but he suddenly tensed

as he swung the wheel of the jeep and it did not respond. We hit the bus exactly head on. The horn, too late, began to howl.

After a while I became aware that we were embedded under the bonnet of the bus, and that the soldiers on either side of me were gravely hurt. Nobody moved for some time, except the refugees who plodded slowly round our debris; it meant no more to them than anything else; this was someone else's calamity, and they were too numbed to trouble.

By and by a police truck came by and found me sitting in the red slime on the roadside, and helped me into Krishnanagar, and by then I had really had enough.

It was not a good road back to Calcutta and the driver was not anxious to dally through ninety miles of Bengal in the darkness; after a while of jolting the pain became quite bad. I do not recall talking about anything on the way. Finally we rolled up the silent Chowringhee past the closed cafés and the pavement-sleepers and reached the hotel about three in the morning.

The driver covered me with an old macintosh to hide my appalling clothes; I was so soaked and matted with the soldiers' blood that I feared the night-clerk at the desk would invoke some regulation and refuse to admit me. As it was I must have appeared grotesque enough, blundering and stumbling in supported by the driver's shoulder, and the hotel clerk slid my key across the desk with obvious distaste; at that time in the morning he must have concluded that I was very drunk. Somehow or other I got manhandled upstairs to the room. I cut off my filthy clothes with a razor-blade, very slowly and painfully, and lay on the bed to consider what might next be done. I fell asleep at once.

When I woke up in daylight I simply could not move at all. I felt as though I had been jumped on by an elephant.

It seemed clear enough that I had broken one leg and not improbably both; one kneecap seemed to be on the wrong side. The left of my rîbcage appeared to be one immense soggy bruise, and my back from the buttocks to waist had no feeling at all. The situation presented a dilemma.

For nearly twenty-five years I had had a singularly haunting horror of being ill in Calcutta. Of all places in the world it would be the worst nightmare for personal sickness; Calcutta, dedicated for generations to the maintenance of suffering, is necessarily the most indifferent to it, quite apart from the fact that in all of West Bengal there is scarcely one hospital bed for every thousand people. Moreover I feared being ill in Calcutta because once it had happened to me.

Long before, some time in the late 1940s, I had come to Calcutta from South India, travelling by stages up the eastern coast. In those days there was much primitive accommodation; by night one shared it with clouds of winged things, and the thin whine of the mosquito then was often that of the anopheles. By the time I reached Calcutta the malaria had incubated well; as we jogged along in the wooden bus from Dum Dum airport through the dusk, through the flaring lamplit squalor of the suburban slums, through miles of flickering clamorous streets, through banks and strata of turbulent sounds and smells, the ride took on more and more the quality of my own fever; we seemed to be threshing wildly deeper into the core of some surrealist delirium.

I walked in a heavy daze into the gaunt hotel – the same in which I found myself today, now so transformed – which made no impact on my mind but the throb of what seemed to be many unrelated dance-bands of blaring dissonance, into a wooden room, on to a rocking bed.

Only one incident remains : as I dripped into the deeper confusions of the fever I was further distracted by two realisations, or rather one that was concomitant to the other. First that I was going to die, which seemed of little consequence except for the fact that I had omitted to register in the hotel, nor had I been able to send a routine telegram. Therefore no one in the hotel, indeed no one in Calcutta, nor for that matter anyone anywhere, could possibly know who I was. They would find me, and after some desultory enquiry would shrug me off and heave me incognito on to one or another of the congested burning-ghats of this starving city. I tossed around resentfully at the thought of this ultimate anonymity, but I did not appear to have the resolution to do anything about it. I began to dream of gallons of soda-water, oceans of it lapping to my chin and down my burning throat.

The doctor who eventually arrived – I never learned exactly how or why – recounted sardonically how he had come into the bleak room of the hotel and found it littered, scattered wildly everywhere with sheets of copy-paper, on the bed, the floor, the table; on each sheet were scrawled only the two words of my name.

'Something of an egoist,' he had suggested with professional good humour. I had found it impossible to explain how wholly wrong his theory was, how completely contrary an emotion had been involved.

And now I was back in the same place, and in rather worse case. This was evident because Calcutta itself was clearly in worse case. At best one needed all one's health and strength to cope with the wretchedness of this hopeless place; now its concentrated unhappiness was even more compounded and congested by the demands of the uncountable refugees it seemed truly unpropitious, not to say churlish, to impose an extra unimportant demand on the overtaxed medical resources. In any case they were becoming very edgy about the likelihood of the spreading cholera, and I had no wish at all to get involved in that.

So I decided to get myself splinted up and sellotaped together in a do-it-yourself way to see if I could make it back to London on my own.

Just as the flight of the bumble-bee is said by experts to be aerodynamically impossible, though it manifestly takes place, so, after it was accomplished, was this long and blundering hobble to the airport and on to London defined as orthopaedically out of the question, though nonetheless it came to pass. Moni's association with the airline eased some of the more troublesome transitions, yet I still remember little of that peculiar journey. It went well: how else could I have found myself two nights later being driven in passing good spirits in an ambulance from the airport to the hospital? There my bones were disposed in more orderly and professional casts. I was home and happy; that, I thought, was the epilogue. It was of course the reverse, but I did not know that then, nor do I think I would have cared much if I had known.

Some time later my heart began to fire on three cylinders, then on two, then one. It was an eerie sensation, like drowning in a dream. Events slid out of my control.

11

THEY CELEBRATED my three score years (giving me a decade's edge on the prophet's allotted span) by sawing through my breastbone, spreading out my carcass in somewhat the manner of a smoked fish, sealing off my vital functions, and slicing the chambers of my heart – in short, causing me technically and temporarily to die so that (as they say on war memorials) others could live. The others, to be sure, included myself, because I do not consider the individual who emerged in the evening gasping and blubbering from this odd experience to be quite the same one who was wheeled upstairs that morning full of pentothal and who, as seems evident, did live.

·This was in fact a matter of some surprise to all concerned. Major open-heart surgery on middle-aged and slightly shopworn journalists was unusual in these days, and the operating staff had very reasonably and considerately suggested that the chances were about three to one against. This was curiously reassuring, in so far as I needed reassurance; by this time I had few emotions about it one way or the other.

*

There was a certain interlude.

I got the impression that I was being moved from place to place, that the habit of a lifetime was being continued as it were by some sort of intrinsic momentum, since I was by now hardly able to stir. I learned later that this had indeed been the case, that these little rides through London with a placid nurse holding a drip-bottle above me had been real enough, and that there were a variety of hospitals, although for what reason I was obliged to travel amongst them I had not the energy to enquire. From the time I was moved into Medical everyone forgot about my leg; that was lost in the orthopaedic past. I was now a Heart, and they could not do enough about it, dosing it, X-raying it, listening to it, shaking their heads over it. One day I said: 'I think my foot is going to fall off,' and when Sister murmured to the houseman he said: 'Of course, of course, he's got a *leg*; better remind them.' When the leg-people came to have a look the heart-people hung fretfully around, glancing at their watches; they were being cheated by an irrelevancy.

One of the wards was a cavernous dormitory full of very old decaying men. Whatever ailed them had seemingly got lost long ago in the simple fact of their decrepitude; they were just mouldering away in various phases of somnolence or petulance, in attitudes of senile inelegance. The nurses handled them with a combination of irony and gentleness that greatly impressed me with its patient humour, for a more tiresome crowd of old devils I had never seen. Those capable of movement were always trying to escape. Three beds from me was a Mr Colebrook, a putty-coloured ancient of days whose whole personality varied from hour to hour. He would at one moment be a prone, still, obviously terminal case, incapable of movement; the moment the coast was clear he would whip a cloth cap from under his pillow and be off, tottering down the ward in his pyjamas.

'Off to California, mate,' he would say, in the few seconds before they intercepted him and led him unprotesting back to bed, where he would again feign catalepsy for an hour or two.

There was a lietmotive all day from the nurses: 'Oh, Mr Spenser; don't do that, Mr Spenser, you're not on the toilet yet; just wait a minute Mr Spenser; oh you are a nuisance, man, you've done it; why can't you ever wait Mr Spenser....'

I have almost reverentially happy memories of most of my hospital wards, but not especially of this one, wherever it was. By night it was a place of groans and barks and mutterings, like a zoo at twiligñt, with now and again a cadenza of curses from one or another semi-conscious old frame, subsiding into snores. In the early morning it looked like an old picture of Buchenwald: livid skeletal faces, open toothless mouths, disarranged beds revealing bony bodies pale-green in colour, bent in the foetal attitude or sprawled in the abandon of death. When the radio news came through the headphones it was now beginning to talk of the Bengal refugees, but nobody listened.

I was very happy when they moved me downtown to the cardiac hospital, which was small and specialist and serene.

The doctors were peevish about it amongst themselves; as they dripped isoprenaline into me they debated whether this now evident aortic stenosis of mine had anything to do with the Bengal accident and the heavy bash on the ribcage. It seemed clinically unlikely; more probably the trauma of the smash had merely revealed a cardiac defect many years old of which I had been unaware, or possibly unwilling to accept because of the erratic and obsessive nature of my life. Had there never been suggestions of such a condition? They asked suspiciously, prompting me with leading questions about swollen ankles and the like.

Well, I could have said, thirty-one years ago HM George V had summarily kicked me out of his armed services for reasons that on an unpleasant and long-forgotten buff form were described as cardiac deficiencies, but one did not take that very seriously. I had just lost a very young wife in childbirth and I was badly disorientated and unmistakably ill; I appreciated that the MOs were unexpectedly compassionate; knowing that I had a ten-day-old daughter to support alone they were playing a generous game. They sent me about my business, recommending that I absent myself in future from onerous situations and activities, and on no account to move above an altitude of three thousand feet. Since that time it had become obligatory to work in almost continually a great variety of highly onerous and disagreeable military situations wearing a variety of curious liveries and passing an inordinate amount of my time travelling at very great heights; it may have disturbed my psyche but it had not damaged my health. Consequently I did not find it necessary to develop this argument with the doctors, who had in any case clearly made up their minds long before.

At all events the question seemed to be growing more academic all the time, since apparently the indications were quick surgery with an aortic valve replacement and the implantation of an electrical pacemaker, and what did I think about that?

What I thought about it was a predictably automatic response : over my dead body would they slice me up. They replied impatiently that slicing up over dead bodies was a notorious waste of time. They paid me the compliment of being very fractious with me indeed. The culmination of the brief debate was that if I argued any longer about slicing up over dead bodies that was precisely what would happen, so they would ask my wife.

It seemed very easy in retrospect. My feelings were so complex yet my perceptions so blurred that I gladly surrendered all initiative, lying there with the electrodes wired to my monitor, bleeping gently away with its gay little graph on the screen, every peak marking another three-quarters of a second of available life. Whenever I winced it responded; it was like having one's own television show.

Somehow the scene changed to the Heart Hospital. Another new doctor arrived and pulled out every one of my teeth.

The shock of this penetrated even my sedation; this I had not expected. I tried to protest through a mouthful of stitches like a wire fence, but I could say nothing.

My wife: 'But you're going to open his heart, why take his teeth?'

Surgeon: 'There it is; I'm sorry, Mrs Cameron, but it's a long and perilous operation; your husband is a man of a certain age; the possible infection of the dental roots is a chance we can't take.... The teeth were lousy anyhow.'

'But every single one? You know he's a vain man....'

'I'm sorry,' said the decent busy man. 'Tomorrow your husband is going to have a lot more to worry about than his teeth.'

It seemed petulant to complain, with the big act closing in. Ordinarily I would have been frightened to death. Indeed I *was* frightened to death. Yet that was the wrong phrase too. I could honestly say, even at that point, that I had never been afraid of death; the consolation of the unbeliever is that he cannot be intimidated by oblivion. But dying, now – that was a different matter. I was somewhat afraid of dying, because I am fundamentally a coward and always mistrusted myself in a situation of pain. I was very uneasy about the indignities of dying; I had seen it happen to so many people abruptly and unexpectedly and clumsily, full of fear and anger, the humiliation that is the really dirty trick of death. My sort of generation had been obliged to assist at the epic glory of death which had too

210

often turned out to be blood and whimpers; I would fain have dodged it, though it was somewhat late to think of that now. Moreover I did not see it presenting much of a problem after I left the ward.

My wife – through those baffling drugged days whenever I surfaced into reality she seemed to be there, like some glowing outrageous intrusion into all that white and chromium; her saris grew more iridescent every day. Sometimes she brought her children who are now mine, Sabita and Kiron, and my own son Fergus. These hours were my days.

Then came the minor fantasy of the blood. The operation, it seemed, required copious fresh blood for transfusion, and my group appeared to be marginally uncommon – except, oddly, among Asians. Miraculously my wife's group matched. In my bemused sentimental state this moved me greatly; it seemed of ritual importance. One pint out of twenty – I urged them to keep my wife's pint until the last so that I would have it in the end, going round forever in my heart.

'Really, Mr Cameron, you overdo this romantic symbolism. The heart is a hollow muscle, a pump....'

In the weeks to come I was to exercise a number of demons within me by writing a radio play (by and by it won the Prix Italia, which was a surprise for my first and last essay in such a field). We called it *The Pump*. It was a new consideration to me.

All these years I took it for granted, I dare say. As hearts go, that is. It bumbled on in its own way and in its own time, seeing round the hours of the day and the seasons of the year without any prompting or argument from me. It was a good old heart, thought I, when I gave it any thought at all.... In this place they don't go much for the romantic concept, I've observed. People do not love each other with all their hearts. Their hearts are neither warm nor cold. The thing is no more central to our physiology than the backside or the bladder. I speak from the heart, Sister. How can a heart be full of love? The heart is a hollow muscle of extraordinary strength; it is a simple pump, pushing round two thousand gallons of blood a day....

They forgave me when I bored them; this was the kind of hospital where they were accustomed to a high level of self-indulgence.

'Auricles, ventricles.... You must know the old classics, doctor, the comedies of Auriculus, the satires of Ventriculus, in the great days of the empire of the Pericardium. And yet' – said I, warming to my tedious work, delaying all these good people from more important tasks, believing with a fair certainty that this was the last opportunity I should have of articulating my half-baked notions – 'on the eve of this personal Grand Guignol my pump *is* full of love. Allow us our dopey dreams, doctor. Allow us to wear our pump upon our sleeve. Blessed are the pure in pump, for they shall see God. But they damn well won't see you.'

The only way they could shut me up was to send me to the catheterising theatre. Two holes in the ankles, two holes in the elbows, and into them the long sinuous inquiring rubber lines, worming their way through the blood vessels while the table rocks from side to side, imperceptibly, until – ah! ah!! – they reach the heart itself. The flexible spies, the scouts, prospecting the battlefield for the knife to come. That could not be worse than this.

In bed again: a feeling of idleness, complicity, fatalism, fear. It was happening to someone else; it was always happening to someone else. Presumably I *was* someone else. Across the ward from me – and it was a very little, companionable ward – was what seemed to be a decent pious

Italian in a state of sorrow; a priest came in and set up his bed-table with a couple of candles and a book and heard his confession. And there myself, in the middle of all this, obliged to piss into my bottle. I meant no offence, but my diuretic pills gave me no chance; when you had to go you had to go, even in the middle of a Hail Mary. Nobody noticed anyway.

The clergyman was not so easily dismissed. I heard him padding over to me and the preparatory clearing of the throat.

'Good day, Mr, ah, Cameron; I don't think we've met. I'm by way of being a chaplain here; honorary of course; we have a small public, Mr, ah, Carter; I don't know if you're one of us?'

'Matter of fact, no.'

'Ah – another persuasion, perhaps?'

'Not really, sir.'

'Ah. I take it, then....'

'I'm not a brand from the burning. I don't even smoulder, really.'

'Very good, very good. After all, I'm only a sort of, ah, amenity here, in case of need.'

'I'm not a candidate for the last rites, really.'

'Dear me, no; *what* an idea.'

'To be frank, sir, men of God make me uneasy. I'm not even an aggressive heretic.'

'Well,' said the clergyman, soothing and defensive, 'for that matter I'm no missionary. Gilbert Chesterton, whom I had the pleasure of meeting as a young man.... My, how that dates one, does it not?'

'He came to supper occasionally with my father when I was a boy.'

'Really? You wear very well, Mr, ah, Cameron.'

'Come back and check next week, Father,' said I cruelly.

'Be sure I will,' he returned the service adroitly, 'or

not, as the case may be. Anyhow,' he went on, rocking on his heels, 'as I was saying, G. K. Chesterton wrote a book years ago in which, as I recall it, he has some sort of a huge symbol of a valley in Wessex, where all those horses and things are carved on the hillside. Then there was this boy, whose cottage lay on such a hillside, who felt obliged to travel the world in search of something very mystical, some enormous effigy or grave of some giant or other – you know what those Catholic intellectuals were in the twenties. And when he'd gone just far enough from home he looked back and saw that his own cottage, flat on the hillside like the quarterings of a shield, was a part of just such a huge figure, on which he's always lived, but which was too big to be seen. His point was, I imagine, that the next best thing to being really inside Christendom is to be really outside it. Like that boy, Mr, ah, Cameron – or yourself, of course. There are doubtless many aspects of my calling on which you have a wider view than I. We must have a little chat some day.'

He was a well-intentioned decent man; I dreaded his reappearance.

I read in a book of Anthony Burgess's essays: 'The late Pope John said that any day was a good day to die. He might nevertheless have conceded that some days are better than others, and that no Christian could ask more than to die on Easter morning – suddenly, without fuss, having just celebrated the truth of Christ's and thus man's redemption.' (He was, as it happened, writing about Evelyn Waugh.)

How one puzzled over these strange considerations, so wholly academic and remote, determined by superstitions one could never sincerely share. Even in this crisis, seeking any philosophy as better than none at all, it was hard to grasp: how could one day of death be better than another? Should I have paid more heed to the Hindu guru when I had the chance? I still cleaved negatively to the late Pope John: if any day was a good day to die, equally any day was a bad day to die. On the night when I had reason to suppose that this would be determined for me I was – as in the circumstances is everyone else, I should imagine – taken by surprise. To leave so much undone would expose oneself to the charge of improvidence – a wastage of work, of love, of effort, of achievement, even of self-explanation, which one had always left to another and more propitious day. Yet to assume that anyone could possibly be bothered to notice was to be pretentious and absurd, and at least one did not want to be absurd. So I wrote some letters, incomprehensibly, on the understanding that if I were in a position to destroy them the next day I would do so.

Night dissolved into morning.

'Sorry about no breakfast.'

'Take the breakfast out to where my teeth are; let them have the fun.'

One more little needle, one among many. I suddenly thought: I am twenty thousand words behind schedule in my work, and slid into limbo.

I must admit that I had not expected to see my father up in that place – or rather hear him; it was hard to determine exactly where he was. He had always been an elusive man, even when he was alive, but he had meant a great deal to me, and it now seemed important to make that at least clear.

'There was such a lot I had to tell you, and Mother of course, but it escapes me. It's being tethered to the ground like this.'

'I shouldn't worry about it too much,' said my father.

'No, but it's the cold. Christ, it's cold. Mother must be really complaining, you know her. But then you're not pinioned here on your back with the cold eating into your chest. You know they're freezing my heart and exporting it to India? Don't tell Mother, it would upset her.'

He became querulous. 'Why do you keep talking about your dear Mother when you know she's dead?'

'But so are you dead, Father. I don't mean to be unkind about it, Father.'

'That's all right,' he said, kindly. 'How long have your Mother and I been dead? Thirty years?'

'You thirty; mother forty-one. I loved you so much, Father, did I ever tell you?'

'Oh yes, in your way. It was such a long time ago. Bless me,' said my father, puzzled. 'How old are you now, son?'

It was a strange consideration. 'Just about five years older than you, Father.'

'Fancy that,' said my father, admiringly. 'Are you dead too, son?'

'I don't know exactly,' I said truthfully. 'I think they're going to tell me by and by.'

'Who are?'

'These people. These men in the green overalls and the masks invisible against the steel and the lights. They are doing the most extraordinary things to me; I imagine I'm not supposed to know. They are sawing through my breastbone and bending back my ribs with clamps to get at the chambers of my heart.'

'Vampires!' said my father brusquely. 'What demonology is this?'

'The idea is they're saving my life, old man. Kind hearts are more than coronaries.'

'A likely story,' said my father. He, with reason, had gravely mistrusted doctors. 'Do you know what they did to me?'

'Yes, Father, and I don't want to remember it now,' I said, because I had a feeling of impending climax. 'You weren't selfish when you died. Just indulge me now like you always did. Can you see what they're up to?'

'Dear boy, I don't even know where they are.'

'Nor where we are?'

'No, not that either,' he said very sadly. 'It seems like a very long way from home.'

All over me the monsoon rain came pouring down. The frame of vision vertically overhead became full of Bengali faces, gaunt and expressionless, passing across from left to right. Someone was chanting.

'Five million two hundred and eighty-one thousand three hundred and two; five million two hundred and eighty-one thousand three hundred and three; five million two hundred and eighty-one thousand three hundred and....'

The Colonel gave me a friendly clap on the shoulder and put me in the jeep. The curtain of rain came down and we drove straight into the bus. The steel face of the bus continued on straight through my thorax and out the other side.

It is clinically and physiologically impossible that I could have heard the surgeon murmuring through all that hysterical Indian chatter and the thudding of the rain, but I was to hear what he said so often in times to come that to me I heard it then, as I lay there beside the wheel of a jeep in the mud that was yet at the same time on the hospital theatre table in Marylebone.

'From now on the cardiac and respiratory functions are arrested, circulation and breathing are now assumed by the heart–lung machine. That is to say, the heart and the lungs are now by-passed and their operation is taken over, as you know, by the apparatus by which comparable colder blood is circulated. I remind you that a heat-exchange system is now markedly reducing the body temperature, since the colder the tissues become the less oxygen is required to maintain the life of a cell. And, to be sure, the life of a patient. We are in effect refrigerating him. The patient is therefore technically in a form of suspended animation while we proceed with the mechanical surgery of the implantation. You might call this the critical part....'

But he could not contend against the rain and this shrill Bengali computer-voice in my other ear. 'Five million three hundred and ninety-two thousand and sixty-one; five million three hundred and ninety-two thousand and sixty-two....'

'Nobody will believe you anyway. Nobody will believe me. That six millionth statistic will be an anonymous dead body drifting down the canal.'

'But of course; when has it not been?'

'What, then, am I?'

'Six million a hundred and one; six million a hundred and two; six million a hundred and....'

The shock of the collision – still repeated nightly in my dreams – sent my father spinning back to limbo, and sent me hours later blundering back to life in the recovery-room, fighting the unnatural beat of the respirator with its ruthless rhythm: in, gasp; out, gasp. For a while that occupied all the concentration I could muster. But *cogito*, *ergo sum* – I think, therefore I am; that was something. A great butterfly appeared for a moment at the edge of my field of vision – my wife: I had no means of communication when of all times I wanted it most. She vanished, everybody vanished, and the monsoon rain went on and on.

*

And that, I suppose, was that. I was in hospital a long time. They opened me up, they spread me out, they put in my artificial plastic valve and my electric pacemaker, they closed me up with steel pins and silver wires. I was held

218

together by rivets and activated by a battery like a Japanese toy. To begin with it was very strange.

Anyone who has had his sternum sawn open and his vascular system re-bored will not have to be told that it is not fun. For the first weeks I reflect that I was alive, and every day when my wife came by I knew the nature of the resurrection. It cannot be denied, however, that for a while it hurt worse than hell, and I wept with self-pity quite a lot when alone because, old as I was, I was unused to captivity, and this was a singularly penetrating pain. I did not really understand then how much more desolating this sort of thing is for one's family than for oneself. When I realised this I gave up moaning; this was very therapeutic.

Most of the time I gave no thought to anything at all: darkness alternated with light; there were moments when I felt the sense of liberation that comes to very sick people in kind and professional care: that somehow a burden had been taken away, that no further desperate effort could be required of me again; that I was in a sense freed from the exigencies of a tedious and inadequate body from which I had now taken all that it could provide. This was a new relationship between myself and my physical shell, at the same time a relief and yet deeply grievous, as though parting with an old companion that had given one some pleasure in its time and perhaps would not again, or in the same way. It was hard to say why this should be. No more midnight telephone calls, no more desperate dashes to the airport, no more futile and frightened pursuits of the gunfire, no more brief encounters foolishly resolved; had I not always waited for this day? There was a gnawing regret that the time had not been of my choosing: no more.

So there I lay as the days went by, and as the nights went by, which strangely enough were more vivid and startling, for then the nightmares were always waiting

219

round the corner, with the monsoon rains pouring down on the refugees and the great iron prow of the bus forever roaring nearer, the cruel metallic thing that was now embedded in my chest. At these times I could never quite understand where I was nor how I had come to be there, and brief panics took over. These moments were assuaged by women profoundly practised in patience.

Gradually I became aware of them, first as a simple uniformed order of beings dispensing discipline and consolation equally and with a sure hand, then, more slowly, as individuals, as women of what my passing gratitude took to be of truly surprising beauty, both of appearance and nature. I took to reflecting on how this should be: why should girls so clearly capable of easier and simpler lives commit themselves to this hard and tedious and ill-rewarded routine? How did these fresh and starched young things, white and black and brown, retain their good humour, even gaiety, in their dealings with these boring and demanding bedridden strangers, performing for them the most sordid offices with such incomparable goodwill and, sometimes, even laughter?

In the days when the nightmares were always waiting for the darkness a night-sister stood between me and them, with at bad times a pill and at less bad times a cup of tea. I did not know what the medicinal value of a cup of tea was; tea was as meaningless to me then as it had always been, but its arrival in the baleful green glow of the night-light was an act of grace. In my mind I wrote lines for a sister's soliloquy:

'Our creatures,' I made her say, 'our merchandise, our pets, our patients. We love them, we act them up, we're wily and deceitful and kind. They love us and loathe us; they flinch from our approach and they long for the touch of our hands. Never a heartbeat but we know it, or are supposed to; never an arterial pressure nor a mouthful

220

drunk nor a secretion lost but we put it in a book; never a milligramme of antibiotic that isn't on the record; how they need our vigilance, how they must hate our curiosity. If this man dies tonight the last thing he will have known is my tiresome insistence that he stay alive. I really don't know why.'

Every evening my wife came in – a jug of fruit juice, a bottle of wine, a plate of cheese – adding to her own weariness at the end of a working day to see me fed and watered; I lived for that hour. Messages of kindness and encouragement came in from everywhere – including, unexpectedly and happily, an enormous telegram from Archbishop Makarios, of all people, compounding the fantasy of the time.

After some time they gave me a rope with one end tied to the foot of the bed and the other within my grasp, by hauling upon it with my arms I was able to lift the upper part of my body into a more sociable position; thus I was able to receive my guests, who were more properly my hosts, since it was they who brought me what I needed. I balked at flowers; I could never understand the consoling purpose of cut flowers in hospital; beautiful objects so visibly condemned to death, diligently arranged in funerary vases so that their daily withering would insist upon mortality, both theirs and mine. I entreated people not to bring me flowers, so deeply did their decay depress me. Instead I begged for oddities like scraps of nursery food, pap and slop that I could eat with my ruined and toothless mouth. The loss of my teeth in many ways affected me more than the loss of my aortic valve; it was more directly troublesome, ugly and embarrassing. I could conceal my long thoracic scar but not my face. I avoided as far as possible looking in the mirror at this grotesque metamorphosis of a countenance, now collapsed into the likeness of a Dürer drawing of an old man. The new situation also presented serious problems of eating. The food in the hospital was as wretched as its every other aspect was superlative, but even had it been *cordon bleu* it would have been difficult. I grew into the custom of living on interesting and diverse scraps brought in from outside, like a privileged political prisoner. Thus I subsisted for a considerable time on ripe Stilton cheese and a fine concoction prepared by Moni out of milk and egg and whisky. In fact I thrived on it; I acquired the custom of living on a great variety of titbits at odd and intermittent times. To this day I have a reluctance to eat formal meals in the company of others, preferring to steal small portions of food from the refrigerator and whisk them away into privacy; I developed the gastronomic habits of an alley cat.

*

In the end my legs seem to have got better on their own, having given up the competition for sympathy.

So I was sent away a mended man. For a brief moment I went through the valley of the shadow, as many a better man has done, and at the end of the tunnel I found everything there much the same as before. I was a bit lame, but that was merely my legs being resentful. I did not gambol upstairs. The pacemaker attended to its business and provided proof of its usefulness some seventy-odd times a minute; only at moments of impatience did I feel that I was slightly pregnant with a can of soup. The plastic valve (as my witty surgeon pointed out) was the youngest part of my body and quite the most durable. The curious ticking noise it made in the night was furthermore a kind of moral guarantee, since anyone unfamiliar with this ticking would be liable to spring from the bed crying: 'For God's sake what's that noise; it's the IRA; we've got four minutes before you go off!' Such simple jokes were the measure of my redemption.

I now began to work as hard as ever. No, that exaggerates, but nearly as hard. I had always been a writer to trade, and most of my life I was a foreign journalist, spending years in ceaseless travel about the planet, usually at the times of its more spectacular tribulations. This I might no longer do, or at least less feverishly. I was intending in any case to career around less, and now I had a foolproof excuse. I was uncommonly fortunate in being able to earn a living sitting on my backside – not perhaps as ample a living now, but more easily. I had a wife who gave me not only her life's blood, but my life's hope.

I accepted a way of life that required regular attention at an Anti-Coagulation Clinic, where one made friends rather as one did in the old London war-time fish-queues: affable strangers with a common purpose. I was obliged to eat each day some six or seven milligrammes of warfarin, which is poison to rats but good for me, and this I would have to remember to do for the rest of my life. Instead of smoking eighty cigarettes a day I could now smoke none. (This was an onerous discipline I am obliged to admit, and I bragged about it immoderately.) I continued to drink whisky, as I was allowed to do, though markedly less than before, and about time too. I took shameless advantage of my circumstances by letting my family and friends do things for me that I could perfectly well do for myself.

I never met my father since. Not so the refugees.

I left the hospital walking on air, in so far as one can walk on air with a heavy stick, yet with a paradoxical sense of regret. I have been back there so many times since; I cannot be the only man who returns there without doubts or dreads. It had been for me a place of great unhappiness and fear, where I had learned the acceptance of pain as an unremarkable norm of life, and its occasional retreats as

223

extraordinary pleasures to be savoured and enjoyed. I had discovered the frustrations and anxieties of being banished from useful work of the only kind I knew. And yet the end of that Indian summer in the hospital is associated in my mind only with the compassionate disciplines and gentle generosity of patient people who owed me a great deal less than I owe them.

When I was released back to the house in which we then lived in Chiswick the first fact of which I became physically aware was that the stairway to the bedroom had no banister-rail, a thing I had never noticed before. Having nothing to hold on to made an unexpected difference. Thus I began to come to terms with new factors of dependence in the ordinary affairs of life. Things hitherto irrelevant acquired a meaning: that they should not be too low to stoop for nor too high to reach for, that the Underground station is no longer five minutes away but fifteen, that an hour's delay in the arrival of the newspapers is not an irreparable loss, that every day's awakening to a new morning is indeed to a new life.

Good luck took its time in coming, but it came.

*

Far away in India it is now sundown, the cow-dust hour. Their feet will be raising the blue-grey haze among the trees and against the dusk, the haze from a hundred supper-fires filling the air with the smell of coming night. Half of me is there still.